Easy Edibles

NUMBER FIFTY-THREE
W. L. Moody Jr. Natural History Series

Easy Edibles

How to Grow & Enjoy Fresh Food

JUDY BARRETT

TEXAS A&M UNIVERSITY PRESS *College Station*

LIBRARY OF CONGRESS CATALOGING-IN-PUBLICATION DATA

Barrett, Judy, 1945– author.
  Easy edibles : how to grow and enjoy fresh food / Judy Barrett.—First edition.
     pages cm—(W. L. Moody Jr. natural history series ; number fifty-three)
  Includes bibliographical references and index.
  ISBN 978-1-62349-339-4 (flexbound : alk. paper)—
  ISBN 978-1-62349-343-1 (e-book)
  1. Food crops. 2. Gardening. 3. Organic gardening.
I. Title. II. Series: W.L. Moody Jr. natural history series ; no. 53.
  SB175.B37 2015
  635—dc23
                    2015014269

Contents

Preface

Nothing is more obvious than our dependence on food. Without it, we die. Period. Food is life and sustenance and all that, but it is also delicious, yummy, pretty to look at, and a pleasure to consume. Yet we approach our food with an amazing casualness. We play with it. We get scared of it and blame all our woes on it. We define ourselves and others by what is on a plate, and we sometimes stick our noses in the air and declare our superiority based on what's for dinner. We gorge ourselves on it. We allow strangers to control the quality and production of everything we eat. Shockingly, we even throw away about 40 percent of our food in the United States every year at the same time that more than 50 million Americans struggle to feed themselves. Looking forward, scientists say food shortages could be the most critical world issue within 40 years—too many people, not enough food production.

All of those things need to change, from the frivolous to the serious, and I think they are changing. People are enjoying food more, talking about problems relating to food, and helping others who need help. One way to help yourself in many ways is to grow a little of your own food. The results are tasty, being outdoors is good for you, and the sense of satisfaction and accomplishment is indescribable. I think we need to simplify our ideas about food—it is good, enjoyable, and essential. And it can be a lot of fun to grow your own. Obsessing isn't necessary; dirty hands are.

This book is designed to encourage people to grow even a little of their own food and have a good time doing it, and on a broader scale, to be aware of who else is growing it. Without the help of gardeners, farmers, and other people involved in the huge task of feeding a voracious population, none of us could get by. I am grateful to all of them for teaching me, feeding me, and sharing with me.

I am also grateful to my family, who keep me interested in feeding them and myself well. I am especially happy to have grandchildren who cheer me up, help me out, and make me hopeful for the future. Pictures in this book of Bailey, Braxton, Ella, and Trenton demonstrate how much fun and how productive gardening can be for young and old. They not only posed for photos but were positive influences in the garden and hardworking helpers.

Special thanks go to the people who shared their wonderful photographs that make this story come to life:

Renee Shepherd, Renee's Garden Seeds, California
Linda Lehmusvirta, producer, *Central Texas Gardener*, KLRU TV, Austin
Tim Mann, Friendly Aquaponics, Hawaii
Karen Wilkens, Master Gardener, Burnet County, Texas
Carol Ann Sayle, Boggy Creek Farms, Austin, Texas
Letitia Pierce, Garden Anywhere Box, Oklahoma
Cheryl Houghtaling, a friend of the farmers' market in Brownsville, Texas
Saundra Winokur, Sandy Oaks Olive Orchard, Elmendorf, Texas
And of course, Bob Helberg, photographer on demand and cheerful fellow-traveler. All photos not credited to someone else are his and mine.

Easy Edibles

1 Is This Going to Be Hard?

If you tremble at the thought of growing your own food, you're not alone. The thought of growing every bite that enters your mouth is pretty daunting. After all, farming is hard work, requires a lot of land, takes up all your time, and leaves you at the mercy of wind, rain, heat, cold, and critters of all kinds. The good news, on the other hand, is that growing some food can be positively enjoyable. It gives you a chance to spruce up your yard, get outdoors with the people you like or all by yourself depending on your preferences, soak up some sunshine vitamin D, and stretch out those stiff muscles that have been staring at screens of all sizes for too long. And that doesn't even include the smile that will

Bailey moving compost.

Ella, Trenton, and Braxton dig in.

spread across your face when you pop a ripe strawberry, tomato, or tender pea into your mouth. So, relax. You've got this! It's going to be fun.

History Is Long

Not many generations ago and extending back to the hunters and gatherers, people grew most if not all of their own food. Adam and Eve might have found their garden all planted and ready for harvest, but most folks had to do the work themselves. My maternal grandfather worked for the railroad, but he always raised at least one hog per year and a large garden to feed himself, his wife, and their six children. My paternal grandfather worked for the post office, but he also had a large garden and had nine children to feed. Both of them lived in town and devoted what space they had in their backyards to raising food. My grandmothers both had rosebushes in the front yard and some cut flowers among the onions, but food was the essential garden choice in the first half of the twentieth century in rural Texas.

The United States was a country of farmers in the beginning, and agriculture was part of everyone's life until recent times. Even the most important members of society had to be involved to some extent in growing food. Michelle Obama is not the first to plant food at the White

House—not by a long shot. Abigail and John Adams, the first inhabitants of the White House, planted fruits and vegetables to feed their family in 1800. If George Washington had lived in the White House, he surely would have planted a garden as well. He was an enthusiastic gardener/farmer. In spite of the fact that early Washington, D.C., was something of a swamp, the first families persevered. Thomas Jefferson added ornamentals and fruit trees to the Adamses' garden and planted his own extensive vegetable garden in Charlottesville in anticipation of his retirement. He inspired other Americans to plant gardens in their yards and continues to inspire us with the historic gardens at Monticello, where heirloom plants are grown, propagated, and shared. John Quincy Adams personally planted fruit trees, herbs, and vegetables to support his household. Through the years, first families have continued the tradition. During World War I, the Wilsons brought sheep to graze on the lawn and fertilize while they munched around the grounds. Eleanor Roosevelt planted a victory garden during World War II and set the tone for millions of Americans who followed suit. About 40 percent of America's vegetables during World War II came from home gardens.

Throughout their lives, both my parents loved fresh food. They bought vegetables from truck farmers in the area when fresh produce was in season and were willing for farmers to settle their bills with a big pile of green beans. Mother always put in a tomato plant or two in a flower bed and had a plum tree in the yard. Daddy got interested in grafting pecan trees for a while and dug up a little plot for me to plant seeds of my choice. And of course, they went to Safeway to buy most of their produce and were happy it was there!

I am also happy that HEB and Sprouts are just down the road to provide most of my family's groceries. Growing all or most of the food you need to feed your family involves hard physical labor, unreliable weather, unpredictable pests, and a whole array of circumstances that can foil your best-laid plans. Farming is a lot riskier than, say, betting on the ponies. Not only is farming hard work, but once you have grown the food, dealing with it is also hard work. "Putting up" vegetables, fruit, and meat involves big pots, lots of heat, heavy lifting, and careful preparation. Having a small home harvest, however, allows for fun—making bread-and-butter pickles, jelly, herb salts, and other nifty additions to the

pantry. What was once heavy lifting becomes a pleasure and another source of pride and satisfaction. Nothing gleams like jars of brilliantly colored jelly!

Memory Is Short

As people moved away from the farm in the middle of the twentieth century, they forgot some of the satisfaction that came with growing their own food. Some even forgot how good a homegrown tomato could taste! It is heartening to see that many of the most enthusiastic "foodies" today are young people who are just discovering the difference between a just-picked peach and one that has traveled thousands of miles from the farm to the store. Questions of food safety, poisonous pesticides and herbicides, genetically modified organisms (GMOs), and other issues are of concern to many people and worthy of note and inquiry, but one of the most important things to me is to maintain that connection between ourselves and what sustains us.

Why Bother?

We are fortunate to live in a time when we have so many choices. Among our choices are those related to food. We can find almost any fruit or vegetable in stores year-round. We can eat watermelon in the snow and fresh green peas at the height of summer. We can choose to grow all our food, some of our food, or none of our food. Why, then, are more and more people opting to seek out local sources of food, including food from their own backyard?

The concerns about poisons used in growing food and the risk of contamination in food processing have made many people rethink the healthiness of food produced by big agriculture. In addition to chemicals used in the United States, food producers in other countries use products banned in this country. In Central and South America, where the seasons are opposite ours, summer crops are being produced to be sold in the winter in grocery stores in North America. From 1992 to 1994, the United States exported 344 million pounds of hazardous pesticides;

Photo courtesy of Boggy Creek Farms

at least 25 million pounds of those pesticides are illegal to use in the US agriculture industry. Most Central and South American growers, however, are free to use these chemicals in any way they see fit and as often as they like. Tomatoes grown in the Culiacán Valley of Mexico, for instance, are treated as many as twenty-five times with chemical pesticides and fertilizers before being shipped to the United States. When you shop, you can usually find the country of origin on the produce boxes. "Product of Mexico" or "Product of Chile" may not necessarily indicate that illegal chemicals are on the produce, but again they may. You just don't know for sure.

Knowing where your food comes from—who grows it, who processes it, who sells it—can go a long way in providing peace of mind that the food you eat is healthy and safe. If you grow your own or buy from local growers, you will know or can find out which chemicals are used, what practices are common, and how long it takes from plant to plate.

Production is under way for a food substitute that will take away all that concern about food, but so far I'm not interested. The idea of a jar

Ella thinks strawberries are better when she grows them herself.

Cucumber. Photo courtesy of Renee's Garden Seeds.

of something tasteless and textureless that will replace all real food just doesn't appeal to me. Instead, I am cheered by the words of Wendell Berry: "If you eat, you're involved in agriculture." The food choices we make extend beyond our kitchens, our grocery stores, and even our own communities. The more options we have, the better. Lots of people growing food means more prosperity, more choices, and more food.

So, there are a lot of reasons to grow some of your own food or seek food grown organically by others in your area, but once more we ask the question: Is it going to be hard? The answer is not only no but heck no! This is going to be fun!

Growing some of your own fresh food is not hard. In addition to that, it is fun and tasty, impresses your friends, and is economical, healthy, and smart! You don't have to spend hours in the field to have delicious fresh produce. You don't have to devote all your free time to plowing, weeding, spraying, and harvesting. You can get a breath of fresh air, stretch your tense muscles, enjoy the encouraging earthy smell of rich soil, and save a trip to the grocery store.

You have a lot of options. That's what this book is about—choosing the ways to get fresh local food that are appealing to you and that work in your life. You can have one flowerpot with something edible in it, or you can share a community garden plot with your next-door neighbor, or you can build an aquaponic system on top of the picnic table. Grow a little; grow a lot. You get to choose and have fun doing it. We are lucky to have so many choices to make sure that the food we eat is good for us and for our families. One way to do that is to grow our own.

2 Working with What You've Got

One of the hardest things about farming is the preparation of the planting beds—plowing, fertilizing, weeding. Enthusiastic (young) gardeners talk about the benefits of "double digging," and I'm sure there are many, but even single digging can wear you out, take up a lot of space, and require dedication and time that many of us don't have.

Adding Vegetables to Existing Landscapes

The smart way to grow a little homegrown produce is to use the space you already have in your yard that is not covered with grass. Most of us have some flower beds around the house or along a fence where we grow

An old iron chair serves as a trellis for cantaloupe plant sharing a bed with Mexican oregano, garlic, verbena, and daisies.

shrubs or perennial and/or annual flowers. These spots could just as easily be home to herbs and vegetables. Once you start thinking of ways to incorporate food into your landscape, you will see opportunities all over the place.

One of the first things gardeners learn, much to our disappointment, is that everything won't grow everywhere. The Internet, magazines, and books all show us gorgeous plants that produce wonderful food, but they often fail to mention that those plants hate cold or hot weather, drought, rainy weather, or some other characteristic that describes our own backyards. Before planting any plant, especially one you didn't buy locally, try to find out what its requirements are in terms of climate, water, and soil. Some plants such as okra and watermelon require long periods of hot weather to produce well. Others such as rhubarb and cress like short, cool seasons. Even different varieties of the same plant can have a certain amount of pickiness when it comes to climate. Brandywine tomatoes, for example, are tasty and lovely big fruits that developed and flourished in relatively cool Pennsylvania. In hot climates the bushes are apt to grow big and tall, and the fruit is likely to be scarce. The best way to learn what will work in your garden is to talk to people who have experience gardening in your area. Talk to Master Gardeners, neighbors with nice gardens, the local extension service, and the employees of local nurseries. Look for local publications (books, newspapers, magazines, and blogs) that are specific to your clime. Of course, you can try anything once, but taking that extra step to do a bit of research will lead to more success and less frustration in the long run as you begin to add edibles to your landscape.

Choosing Herbs as Shrubs, Borders, and Ground Covers

Consider, for example, those evergreen bushes that just sit there and take up space. Can you replace them with rosemary? Rosemary blooms and attracts beneficial insects to your garden, and it adds great flavor to many dishes. You can make tea out of it when you have a cough or cold, and you can rinse your hair with rosemary tea to make your tresses sparkle. The word is that just smelling rosemary improves your mental capacity and memory. Can a wax-leaf ligustrum do any of that?

Rosemary thrives outdoors in US Department of Agriculture (USDA) hardiness zone 6 and higher depending on the variety you choose. It is drought tolerant and will be just fine without extra water for a good long time. Even if you live in cold areas, you can enjoy the benefits of rosemary by growing it in a container and protecting it when the temperature dips.

Upright rosemary bushes love sun and heat. They can grow happily in poor soil or along driveways or walkways where reflected heat is often too much for other plants. They need very little water, fertilizer, and attention. Once the bush is planted, it will grow happily on its own. The only requirement is that the soil drains well. Rosemary cannot live in soggy soil.

A bay tree grows happily in an existing flower bed and blocks the view of the neighbor's garage.

Another great herb that makes a fine landscape plant is the bay laurel (*Laurus nobilis*). Bay makes a nice small tree or large bush in warm climates. The bay leaf is used as a seasoning for soups and stews (and doesn't just come dried in a jar). The tree itself is a nice compact plant that is hardy at least through USDA hardiness zone 7 and can also be grown in a container as a specimen plant. It is generally tolerant of temperatures down to 23°F if it is grown in the ground and can tolerate even lower temps when it is in a spot protected from the wind. (If you don't know which zone you live in, check online for a map.) You can trim your bay tree into a topiary or let it sprawl. It is generally evergreen and a very easy-to-grow, drought-tolerant, pest-resistant, forgiving plant. It will grow in most soils, in sun or part shade, and with very little input from you.

Bay leaves are extremely useful in a variety of ways. They add nice subtle flavor to beans, rice, and other dishes that cook a long time. Unlike many herbs, bay can stand up to heat and will continue to be flavorful after hours of simmering. Also, unlike many herbs, however, bay leaves don't soften when cooked, so it is best to add them to the compost heap once the dish is finished. A bay leaf added to your flour storage container will discourage weevils. If you add a leaf to your rice storage, it will not only protect from invaders but give the rice a nice mild flavor. Bay leaves also discourage roaches in your pantry, so toss a few into the corners. Bay leaf wreaths are decorative, easy to make, and lovely year-round. You can also pluck leaves from the wreaths to toss into the soup without having to go outdoors.

If you live in a very cold climate, you might want to consider adding a juniper bush or two to your garden. Common juniper (*Juniper communis*) is a small evergreen tree or bush that produces seed cones that have been used in food and medicine for centuries. It can take arctic cold and continue to prosper. The seeds, a.k.a. "juniper berries," are very strong tasting, so they must be used sparingly and are most often dried before use. They are the flavoring used to make gin, although we are not suggesting you take up making bathtub gin in your spare time. The berries are also used to flavor meat, particularly strong-flavored meat like venison and other wild game, including game birds. German cooks use juniper berries to flavor a hot sauerkraut and sausage dish that is popular in cold weather. The berries also have a long history of use as medicine in many cultures. However you use them, be sure to begin by using a very small amount. The flavor is strong and can turn a good bird bad in no time.

Herbs make wonderful landscape plants that serve both as decoration and as food. Chives, either onion or garlic, look a lot like monkey grass or liriope along the edge of beds, but unlike their decorative distant relatives, they are tasty and useful in making your food more flavorful and nutritious. Instead of adding more salt, fat, or sugar to your dishes, try adding herbs. Herbs intensify the flavors without adding calories or other unwanted elements. Onion chives (*Allium schoenoprasum*) bloom with bright pinky-purple flowers, and both the leaves and the blossoms are edible and have a mild onion flavor. Garlic chives (*A. tuberosum*) have white flowers and flat leaves rather than round ones like those of onion chives. Society garlic (*Tulbaghia violacea*), another distant relative, has a gorgeous pinky-purple bloom that resembles violets. Its leaves and flowers can be used raw in salads and other dishes. Wild garlic (*T. alliacea*) has edible roots that can be cooked with meats or roasted and then eaten. Society garlic grows taller and has larger flowers than either onion or garlic chives, but all varieties make great borders along a path or at the edge of a bed. In addition to their taste value, these plants help keep pest insects out of my garden and away from the other plants growing nearby. It seems the scent of the herbs confuses the bugs who come in looking for tomatoes or petunias. Chives will grow in full sun or partial shade, especially where the weather is very hot. They require almost no care and will be handy whenever you need a little flavoring for your dinner. Cut the outside leaves back to about ½ inch from the soil; then snip them over your vegetables, salads, potatoes, or whatever else you want them to flavor. The taste of both kinds of chives is mild, so don't add them to a dish that needs long cooking until the very end. They are excellent raw additions to many dishes. The flowers of the onion chives are edible and make a nice vinegar, or they also look splendid floating atop a bowl of soup. Society garlic likes a lot of sun, but it may benefit from late-afternoon shade during the summer. Unlike most garden plants, it is pollinated by moths at night as well as by butterflies and bees during the day. These plants are drought resistant and easy to grow. Garlic chives, when left to flower and produce seeds, will spread all over the garden, so if you don't want more, cut off the blooms before they mature.

Many different herbs can be added to your existing landscape with very little effort. Mint, oregano, and thyme all make great ground covers. If you usually add mulch in the spring to cover the bare ground, stick in a pot of herbs next time. The plants will spread to make a tasty and good-looking green ground cover that grows with minimal attention. In dry climates, thyme does well planted between rocks or pavers to soften the appearance of an otherwise harsh landscape. Thyme loves heat and perfect drainage. Prostrate varieties of rosemary also make good ground covers in places where the soil drains well and the sun shines bright. It is often grown on rocky, hilly spots or inclines near the driveway where the water runs off quickly and the soil stays dry. (If you are afraid you might tumble down the hill as you mow the lawn, plant prostrate rosemary instead and never mow there again!) Oregano and mint are more adaptable to clay soils and occasional sogginess. They can also take more shade than thyme and rosemary.

French tarragon (*Artemisia dracunculus*), long a favorite of gourmet cooks, is a perennial herb that prefers cold weather. Hardy to zones 5 or 4b with protection, it gets too hot in zones 8 and above. Tarragon is a key ingredient in béarnaise sauce and fines herbes (parsley, chives, tarragon, and chervil). It is also a delicious addition to egg dishes, seafood, salad dressings, vegetables, and poultry. Tarragon is a particular favorite of people who enjoy chicken salad. The herb has a sweet, licorice-flavored leaf that is produced on a plant that will grow about 2 feet tall. Find French tarragon plants or take cuttings from a friend's plants. The seeds are highly unreliable. If you see seeds for sale, they are probably for Russian rather than French tarragon. Most cooks think the Russian variety is inferior in flavor. Keep your plants to about 2 feet tall by pruning or harvesting. Use fresh herbs when you can, and freeze some leaves in plastic bags to use in the winter. Tarragon vinegar is also easy to make and a great way to add the taste of the herb to salads and other dishes.

Grow tarragon in a sunny or partly shady spot with well-draining soil. Give the plants room to spread because they produce nice mounding clumps of foliage. Space small plants 2–3 feet apart in the bed. In late fall, water deeply and cover with mulch to protect the roots through the winter. If you live in a hot climate, you can grow Mexican mint marigold as a substitute for tarragon. Some say it is not as good as French tarragon, but it is very similar and smells wonderful.

Herbs in your garden attract beneficial insects and deter pests. Most pests come into your garden based on smell. They are sniffing for things they like to eat, and they don't like the smell of herbs. Many herbs have distinctive fragrances that are attractive to good bugs and annoying to bad bugs. Even deer don't care for the smell of herbs like rosemary and lavender or the shrub Copper Canyon daisy. Butterflies are fond of many herb flowers, and those essential bees that are having such a hard time these days are thrilled to find rosemary and basil plants in bloom. Although herbs won't keep every pest out of the garden, for me, they help.

Your herbal ground cover can be a great companion to other plants in your flower bed. As the pests steer clear of the herb plants, they will also avoid other nearby plants. If you grow herbs near your roses, you will rarely have a pest problem. Herbs have been recommended as companion plants for centuries. There are books written on that subject, but the important thing to remember is that herbs themselves are easy to grow and make other plants grow happily as well. In addition to their companionable nature, herbs can help with the overall look of the garden. If you have spring-blooming bulbs, you need to leave them in place so that the plant can die down naturally and absorb nutrients for next year's blooms, but as that process happens, the plants are less than lovely. As the bulbs die down, however, ground cover herbs are just getting their spring spurt of growth. They will help camouflage the fading greenery of the bulbs. Any herb that escapes into the lawn will just make lawn mowing smell better!

The main goal here is to have fresh food. In addition to an easy-care, attractive yard, you'll have ready-at-hand seasonings to add flavor and zest to your meals. Although many recipes call for chopped herbs, and we see chefs on TV chopping them like crazy, I find it easier to snip herbs with scissors. There are special herb-snipping scissors available with multiple blades, and these are fun and easy to use, but regular kitchen shears are just fine. Using scissors lets you avoid the stems and cut the leaves into small, usable pieces. Grab a handful of mint to add to fruit salads,

Fresh mint is easily snipped with multiblade herb scissors.

tabouli, cucumber slices in yogurt, or the occasional mint julep. Put fresh oregano into your spaghetti sauce, soup, pizza, or pesto. Chopped chives are famous for their use on baked potatoes, but they are also delicious in salads and cold soup, and the pink onion chive blooms make a great vinegar to use with fish. Any of these herbs can be mixed with butter and smeared on toasted bread, on pita wedges, or on bread cubes to make croutons.

VEGGIE AND BEAN SALAD WITH MINT

Make the dressing first and let the ingredients get acquainted while you put the salad together.

    1 clove garlic, crushed

    ¼ teaspoon salt

    2 tablespoons white wine vinegar

    ¼ cup olive oil

    ½ teaspoon dry mustard

    ½ teaspoon cumin

Shake all ingredients in a jar with a lid until everything is mixed well. Let sit at room temperature while you make the salad.

   2 cans garbanzo beans, rinsed and drained
   2 pounds carrots, peeled, cooked, and sliced into chunky pieces
   2 cups walnut halves or chopped walnuts
   ½ cup feta cheese, crumbled
   2 tablespoons snipped fresh mint

Combine beans and carrots with the dressing and toss until the veggies are well coated. Add walnuts, feta, and mint and season to taste with salt. Toss and serve at room temperature.

LEMON CHIVE SAUCE FOR FISH, CHICKEN, OR VEGGIES

   ⅓ cup softened butter
   2 tablespoons snipped chives
   1 tablespoon lemon juice
   1 teaspoon grated lemon zest
   ½ teaspoon salt
   Pepper to taste

Combine all ingredients and spread on hot fish, chicken, or vegetables such as asparagus, broccoli, or carrots. You can also melt the butter to have a pour-on sauce. Surprisingly yummy for such an easy sauce.

ROASTED CHICKEN WITH OREGANO AND/OR ROSEMARY

Rosemary, and oregano, and garlic all go well together. Use what you have and what you like in this simple and tasty recipe.

   4 chicken breast halves or 8 chicken thighs with skin on
   4 teaspoons olive oil
   1 tablespoon snipped oregano or rosemary or a combination
   3 garlic cloves, smashed and minced
   Salt and pepper to taste

Heat oven to 450°F and wash and pat dry the chicken pieces. Make a paste of the olive oil, herbs, garlic, salt, and pepper by hand or in a blender or food processor. Smear some under the skin of each piece of chicken and over the top. Place on a pan sprayed to prevent sticking and bake about 35 minutes or until the temperature registers about 165°F on an instant-read thermometer.

BASIC HERB JELLY

Herb jellies aren't just for toast and biscuits; they also make wonderful glazes for meats and vegetables. Slather the jelly on before or after cooking your dish and enjoy the sweet, fragrant tang it adds. Makes about 32 ounces (four half-pint or eight 4-ounce jars).

> 2 cups of your favorite fresh herb leaves and/or herb flowers*
> 2 cups water, clear juice, or wine (use filtered or spring water)
> ½ cup lemon juice or vinegar
> 4 cups sugar
> Pinch of salt
> ½ teaspoon butter
> 3-ounce pouch of liquid pectin

Pour boiling water (juice or wine) over coarsely chopped herbs and let sit until cool. Strain. You have now made an infusion of herbs.

Combine herb infusion with vinegar**, sugar, salt, and butter in a large, nonreactive pot (stainless steel, porcelain, enamel). Over high heat, bring to a full rolling boil (one you cannot stir down). Stir in the pouch of pectin. Return to full rolling boil and boil for exactly 1 minute, stirring constantly. Turn off heat and pour the liquid into sterilized jars. Screw on clean lids that have been kept in simmering water while the jelly cooks. Turn upside down for a few seconds; then set upright on a clean towel and let cool. The jars should seal as they cool. You can process the jars for 10 minutes in a hot-water bath to ensure that they will last a good long time. Check with home canning books or instructions on the Internet if you haven't done this before.

* Good choices of herbs for jelly are scented basils, bee balm, chamomile, chive blossoms, fennel, garlic, ginger, lavender, lemon thyme, lemon verbena, marjoram, mint, parsley, rosemary, rose petals (white end removed), savory, scented geraniums, sage, tarragon, or thyme.
** Acid to make sure the jelly is safe can be in the form of any kind of vinegar—white or red, cider, wine, balsamic, champagne—or lemon juice. Choose the one that tastes best with your herb.

Most gardeners are familiar with common oregano and its relatives, Greek, Sicilian, and Italian varieties, which grow pretty well in almost all areas of the country. Mexican oregano (*Lippia graveolens*) is from another plant family and makes a lovely small flowering perennial shrub in zone 8. Some report it does well in even colder climes when planted in the ground in a protected spot. It will do well in any climate if it is grown in a container and taken inside in cold winter weather. It grows in full sun or partial shade in almost any kind of soil. The cute little lavender flower is edible and attractive to hummingbirds. The leaves are nicely fragrant and make your spaghetti or pizza pop! This oregano is a native

Mexican oregano blooms throughout the summer.

of Mexico and the Southwest and is widely used in Mexican and South American cuisine. It is also used in folk medicine throughout Mexico.

There are some delicious edible plants that many of us don't even have to plant! These are the ones planted by the birds. Chile pequin (*Capsicum annuum*) is one of the most common of these volunteers. Also known as chile petin, bird pepper, turkey peppers, and other local names, this native of Mexico grows wild throughout the country. The Ladybird Johnson Wildflower Center lists the range of this native to include Texas, Arizona, Utah, and Louisiana as you might expect, but also includes New York, Pennsylvania, Connecticut, and many other northern and central states. It produces very small, bright red peppers that are about ten times hotter than jalapeño peppers. If the birds aren't kind enough to plant these in your garden, you can plant them yourself either from seed or transplant. It you are planting from seed, it is best to plant in the fall as Mother Nature does. You often find these along fence lines where birds plant them while they are resting. They grow happily in part or full shade, and the young green chiles ripen to red throughout the growing season. (The green peppers are hotter than the red.) They will dry to

Native chile pequin pepper is beautiful and very hot.

brown naturally, and you can store them in that state—keep them dry though, or they will grow mold. These little peppers are great in salsa, hot sauces, vinegars, and oils. Any dish you like spicy will benefit from the addition of chile pequin peppers. You can also dry them and then crumble to make sprinkle-on fire. Drop one or two into your soup pot to give the soup a bit more punch.

Remember, despite their very small size, they are hot, hot, hot! Bees, butterflies, and birds enjoy this plant and will frequent your garden doing good deeds when you have it planted there. The bush itself is pretty with bright green pointed leaves and small white flowers that then turn into peppers. The bush can grow in most types of soil and will mature to 2–5 feet tall. Once the seeds or plant are planted, the plant will usually come back year after year even though it is an annual. Generally enough seeds fall to the ground to continue the plant from year to year.

Many gardeners spend a lot of time fighting the yellow wood sorrel plant, a common weed in much of North America. If you are one of those, consider adding the flowers, leaves, or green seedpods to a salad or soup as you would French sorrel. The flavor is sour and strong, so use sparingly, but it is packed with vitamin C. The aboveground parts of evening primroses and spiderworts are also edible. They can be sautéed in butter; added to salads, soups, or stir-fries; or eaten raw. There are other common "weeds" like wild onion and dandelion that produce edible and interesting flavors without your having to do anything but harvest.

In addition to sticking herbs here and there in your flower beds, you can also add fruits and vegetables. Many people plant tomatoes and peppers among the petunias and begonias. They are attractive plants and produce delicious food. Almost everyone longs for home-grown tomatoes in the early summer, so it is common for even the least dedicated gardener to plant a tomato or two in an existing bed, but you don't have to stop there. All vegetable plants are green and pretty when they are growing, and when they are finished, they are easy to remove. You can plant onion starts around the flower beds, in front of the roses, or among ornamentals. These will grow into mature onions, or you can pull them early and use them as green onions. Vining plants like squash or melons will make vigorous ground cover beneath shrubs and bloom nicely as well.

A few years ago I had a volunteer pumpkin come up in a flower bed near the porch. The Halloween decoration had been tossed beneath the rosebushes to recycle into mulch. Instead, it decided to renew into pumpkin. The vine grew happily beneath the roses and then headed out into the lawn. I picked it up and put it back into the flower bed, and it rounded the corner and kept growing. It did eventually grow into the grass, but that was okay with me. It looked really pretty, and it was fun to see the young pumpkins maturing. Once the vine was through producing, I pulled it up and moved it to the compost pile for its next incarnation as plant food. All it takes is a slight mental adjustment. For too long, we've put plants into categories: herbs in the herb garden, roses in the rose garden, vegetables in the vegetable garden, ornamentals in the flower beds. In fact, almost all vegetables are also ornamental. They have pretty green leaves, nice bright blooms, and colorful seedpods (fruit or veggie). There is no reason why these useful plants can't be incorporated into every landscape on the block.

One of the most dramatic plants in my front flower bed is a globe artichoke (*Cynara scolymus*). Several years ago I bought a few small

Volunteer pumpkin was the star of the show in late summer.

A globe artichoke in a front flower bed is a traffic stopper.

artichoke plants in the fall from a local nursery. I put four or five into the raised vegetable beds in the backyard and one in the front flower bed where the soil is fairly poor, the shrubs take up most of the water and nutrients, and I pay very little attention to feeding and watering. You guessed it. The plants in the yummy soil of the vegetable beds died fairly promptly. The one in the front has grown and prospered, multiplied, and produced for years—still in poor soil, still generally untended, and still rarely fed and watered. It grows quietly during the cool months, then becomes huge in early spring and produces more delicious globe artichokes each year. I leave a couple of the artichokes to flower and go to seed. They make terrific purple thistle blooms, and several people driving by have stopped to say, "What is that? It is beautiful!"

Once the weather starts getting hot, the plants die back to a small size until the next winter to start again. What was once one little plant is now a clump of about six plants, all as ornamental as can be—and tasty too! People who live in cool climates can grow artichokes as annuals. They probably won't make it through the winter, but they will produce longer into the summer. Everyone can enjoy this unusual vegetable that is

As the artichoke finishes, a cucumber climbing up a tomato cage comes into its own.

surprisingly nutritious. It contains a good amount of potassium, which is good for heart health, and the phytonutrients and antioxidants in the plant are good for all kinds of things, including a healthy immune system.

Another plant that can easily be tucked into an existing spot in the yard is the Jerusalem artichoke (*Helianthus tuberosus*). Jerusalem artichokes are not from Jerusalem, and they are not artichokes, but at one time a French chef thought they tasted like artichokes, hence that part of the name. In the 1960s Frieda Caplan, a produce wholesaler who was hoping to drum up business for her product, named them "sunchokes." Some people still call them by that name, but whatever you call them, they are attractive, easy to grow, and tasty. The Latin name indicates that these are in fact sunflowers. The bright yellow flowers grow in clusters and have the traditional cheerful daisy look. They grow 4–10 feet tall and are perennials as long as you don't eat all the roots. The tubers are the edible part and contain about 10 percent protein and no starch. They have been promoted as a healthy choice for type 2 diabetics who are yearning for high-carb potatoes. This tuber is high in fiber; some vitamins A, C, and E; and iron.

Plant Jerusalem artichokes in the winter or early spring in a bed that has been freed of grass and weeds. They make a good decorative barrier near a not-particularly-lovely fence or as a hedge between neighbors or to partition off parts of the yard. Plant them about 4 inches deep. Harvest in late fall or early winter. After the first year, there will probably be small tubers left behind to create next year's crop. These tough plants are rarely harmed by pests or diseases. They were grown and enjoyed by Native Americans long before the invention of garden chemicals.

You can eat Jerusalem artichokes raw. Most people peel them, which is sort of a pain because of their knobbiness, but they can be left unpeeled and simply vigorously scrubbed. They are crispy and fresh tasting. Add to salads or use for dipping with other raw vegetables. Add them to stir-fries for a nice crunch. You can also cook them as you would potatoes—steamed, boiled, grilled, fried, or even microwaved. Many potato recipes such as roasted potatoes, potato gratin, and potato salad can be adapted to use Jerusalem artichoke tubers instead.

ROASTED JERUSALEM ARTICHOKES
Preheat oven to 375°F. Coarsely chop as many well-scrubbed tubers as you can eat and drizzle them with olive oil, salt, and pepper. Roast them 35–45 minutes or until soft and golden brown.

Rhubarb is one of those plants that is beautiful and tasty at the same time, so it is a natural for flower beds. Rhubarb is a cool-season perennial that is very winter hardy and resistant to drought. Many northerners who move south mistake Swiss chard with red stalks for their favorite tangy treat, rhubarb. While there have been attempts to develop varieties of rhubarb that will grow well in warm areas of the country, they are not particularly successful. True rhubarb needs a dormant period and a string of temperatures below 40°F to stimulate the next season's growth.

Once established, rhubarb plants remain productive for many years. My husband has fond memories of sitting near his aunt's rhubarb plants, a bowl of sugar at hand, munching on the juicy stalks. He's been known to bring a suitcase full of rhubarb to Texas from Wisconsin after a visit.

Plant rhubarb from roots in well-drained, enriched soil and space them 2–3 feet apart. Don't pick the stalks the first year they are planted, but once they are established, you can harvest by cutting the stalks at the soil line or pull them out one at a time. They are tough plants and don't need a lot of attention, although like most plants will respond well to being fed and watered from time to time. It is best to use the stalks and put the leaves into the compost bin. They contain oxalate, which can cause poisoning in large quantities. That chemical exists in the stalks as well but only in low levels.

Rhubarb is a tangy, sour-tasting plant that is not especially good by itself but is great in combination with other foods. The result is usually a wonderful sweet and sour flavor. Perhaps the most widely known combo is rhubarb and strawberries in pie. Rhubarb is most often used in desserts: pie, cobbler, cake, cookies, and even candy. But rhubarb is a very versatile plant. It can be made into sauces, jams, pickles, and salad dressings and combined into entrées with beef, chicken, fish, and pork.

FISH WITH RHUBARB SAUCE

2 cups rhubarb, cut into small pieces
3 tablespoons olive oil
½ small onion, minced
1 small garlic clove, minced
½ cup tomato puree
½ teaspoon dried or 1 teaspoon fresh basil, chopped
2 teaspoons sugar
½ cup water
Salt to taste
1 pound firm, fresh white fish

Wash rhubarb well. Peel off the hard skin and chop. Heat oil in pan and sauté onion and garlic until they are soft. Add remaining ingredients except fish and simmer about 30 minutes, until rhubarb is cooked thoroughly.

Add cut-up pieces of fish and simmer until fish is cooked. Serve over rice or noodles.

Growing Food in the Kitchen

One group of food you can grow with no yard at all, no extra equipment, and no work to speak of is sprouts. Most of us have a kitchen even if we have no yard or porch. Sprouts are the germinated seed of a plant and include the root and small green beginning of the plant. You want to make sure that the seeds you choose when sprouting are grown without chemicals or other treatment. Certified organic seeds are your best bet. Many kinds of seeds are suitable for sprouting and make tasty additions to your salads, sandwiches, and other dishes. Broccoli, radish, any bean, alfalfa, millet, and wheat are a few of the more popular kinds of seed to sprout. You can experiment with your favorite food seed and see how you like the sprouts. Do not use seeds of the nightshade family—tomatoes, peppers, or potatoes—because they contain some toxins.

To begin your sprout farm, you need seeds and a container with a lid. The size of the container will depend on how many seeds you want to sprout at a time. Generally, ½ cup of bean seeds will produce about 4 cups of sprouts. The container needs to hold the finished sprouts without too much overcrowding. Once you have found your container, you are ready to start.

Soak your seeds in at least twice as much water as there are seeds for 12–14 hours. You can do this in a bowl or pan. Using a colander, rinse the seeds well with cool water. Remove any seeds that have not softened and place the seeds in your sprouting container. Cover them with wet paper towels. Place the container in a warm space and make sure the towels stay moist. At the end of the day, fill the container with water to cover the seeds and let them stand for 15 minutes. Remove the paper towels and pour out the water, using a colander or strainer. Place the seeds back into the container and repeat the entire process for about 4 days (depending on the seeds), beginning with covering with wet paper towels. As you go, check for unresponsive seeds and toss them in the compost. When all the seeds are sprouted, rinse them and they are ready to eat.

Microgreens are a variation on the sprouting idea. They are tiny green plants that are grown quickly and eaten fresh. There are seed mixes especially packaged for microgreens, or you can use your favorite: spinach, lettuce, radish, beet, and any other variety you like. To grow your microgreens, you need a nursery flat, good organic soil, seeds, and a watering device with a diffuser or spray bottle. (You don't want to wash away the soil or the seeds.)

Fill the flat with about 3 inches of soil and then sow the seeds over the surface as evenly as possible. You can mix the seeds with sand for more even distribution. Lightly sift about $1/8$ inch soil over the seeds and press them into the soil. Moisten the soil and keep the seeds in a warm location—indoors or outdoors. Keep the soil moderately moist but not soggy. Once the seeds have germinated, move the flat to a sunny spot. Most microgreens will be ready to eat in about 10 days. Snip off the small plants and use them in salads or on a sandwich.

Both sprouts and microgreens can be grown in almost any season in almost any location. They are fun and easy projects to share with children, and they will produce concentrated taste and nutrition to your diet. Store the microgreens or sprouts in the fridge and eat them while they are fresh.

3 Aw, Grow up!

Do you have a fence? Is there a wall on the garage, on the side of the house, or on a shed that is just sitting there empty? Does your patio, deck, or porch have a rail? You can take advantage of all these elements of your existing landscape to plant some vertical-growing food. Pole beans, vining squash, melons, black-eyed and other southern peas, English or sweet peas, and cucumbers will all be happy to grow up rather than out. While many of these veggies take up a lot of space if they are grown in a standard vegetable or flower bed, when they are grown on an upright support, they take little space on the ground and add beauty to the landscape. Add grapes to this list and you can have your own shady arbor, a covered gazebo, or a fence full of sweet flavor.

Planting on Trellises, Fences, and Walls

Of course, climbing plants need soil in which to grow, but they can grow in the ground to which organic matter has been added or which has been improved through the years, or they can grow in containers with rich potting soil. As long as the container is big enough to hold enthusiastic roots—a 5-gallon pot or whiskey barrel or trough large enough to hold soil and roots—the foliage and flowers and fruit can all go up.

Many of us have fences that partition our yards from the street or the neighbors, and we never think of them as possible trellises. Chain-link or wire fences provide plenty of clinging spots for climbing plants. More solid wooden fences can be crisscrossed with mesh of wire, rope, or other material. As long as there are open spaces where the plants can twine, they will move ever upward. Trellises, of course, are designed for climbing plants and are available at garden centers, antique stores, nurseries, and thrift stores. You can lean trellises against a wall or fence, plant at the base, and watch the plant grow. Climbing plants are programmed to grow toward the sun. That's why you need two plants to go across an arch—one on each side. They will only grow up!

You can buy fan-shaped trellises, wooden lattice that is often used as a decorative element in home building, or steel or vinyl commercial trellises in a variety of styles. Some planters even come with a built-in trellis. You can make your own trellising system from twigs, sticks, netting, string, or wire. More inventive and creative folks have made trellises from bicycle tire rims and spokes, coat hangers, ladders, old doors and windows, and old bed springs. If you enjoy building things, creating clever systems, or just repurposing old things, consider making your own trellis on which tasty treats can flourish.

Italian heirloom squash.
Photo courtesy of Renee's
Garden Seeds.

Veggie Vines

Bean towers or tepees are traditional structures on which to grow beans, peas, or other climbing plants. You can, of course, buy them and set them in a flower bed or corner of the yard. They are usually pyramid shaped and are often very decorative all by themselves. There are also rectangular or square ones available from nurseries and nursery supply stores. If you are so inclined, you can also make your own. One simple method involves buying a bundle of bamboo poles or cutting a bundle of branches from a tree. The pieces of wood should be about 6 feet long and taper from broader to smaller at one end. Push the big end into well-dug soil as deep as you can to give it stability. The best idea is to put the poles in the ground in a circular shape. Then pull the top ends of the poles together and tie them securely with rope or twine. Once your tepee is in place, you are ready to plant.

Another easy-to-make tower involves three poles. These should be 5–6 feet long and made of wood, bamboo, or PVC pipe. Lay the pipes on the ground and mark each of them at 1-foot intervals. Drill holes in the pole at each point. Next, lash the poles together with sturdy twine at the top. Moving down the poles, tie them together in an ever-widening circle so that you end up with a sturdy and stable tripod. Burying the ends of the poles in the soil will make it even more stable.

If you are adding your bean tower to a flower bed or corner of the garden where the soil has not been improved, first dig up the area and work some organic matter into the soil. Compost and/or well-rotted manure are good options. When you have removed weeds, grass, and rocks from the spot and added the amendments, you're ready to place your tower and plant. Bean seeds come in both pole and bush varieties. For growing up, you want pole beans. If you buy at a local nursery, you are sure to find a variety that does well in your climate. They don't all do equally well in every spot. Scarlet runner beans, for example, are beautiful plants and create edible beans, but only in cool climates. In warm areas, they won't produce beans and you'll be disappointed. Southern peas, on the other hand, prefer warmer climates and won't do as well up north. Plant four to five seeds at the base of each leg of the tower. As they begin to grow, help them find the upright around which they can twirl. Once they

Bean Tower. Photo courtesy of Renee's Garden Seeds.

get started, they are ready to take off on their own. After they are a few inches tall, put mulch around the plants to conserve water, discourage weeds, and keep the soil an even temperature.

Beans, of course, are a great choice for bean towers, but you can also grow English peas, southern peas (black-eyed, red-eyed, crowder, etc.), cucumbers, and small melons on your tower. It will look great in your garden and provide a source of fresh food as well as an interesting garden feature. For a little extra flair, you can get a package of bean seeds from Renee's Garden Seeds ("Tricolor") that contains green, purple, and yellow beans. Your tower will be aflame with color!

If you like something unusual on the table and in the yard, consider growing yardlong beans (*Vigna unguiculata* subsp. *sesquipedalisa*) on your fence, trellis, or tower. Also known as long-podded cowpea, asparagus bean, snake bean, or Chinese long bean, this bean is in a different genus from the common bean. This bean, native to Asia, is widely grown and used in that part of the world. It has been available in the United States for only the past several years. The plant is a vigorous climbing

Yardlong beans will grow on a trellis, fence, or any structure that allows them to climb.

annual and produces long pods (14–30 inches, almost a yard) about 60 days after it is planted. The edible pods grow quickly in warm climates and can be eaten fresh or cooked. They are crisp, tender, and tasty. Generally they are cut into short pieces and steamed like regular green beans or used in stir-fries alone or with other veggies. There are several varieties available, but all are very similar in taste and growth habit. Pods are available in purple and green varieties with variously colored seeds.

Yardlong beans are heirloom plants that have proven themselves through generations. They are of little interest to pests and have no common diseases. They also produce longer than the common bean, into the heat of summer. You should plant in different places each year to achieve the best growth. Pick and/or check daily once the beans start growing because they mature quickly and will bear more heavily when they are picked often. They are best when picked before the bean seeds form and when they are less than 18 inches long. Yardlong beans are a good source of protein, vitamin A, thiamin, riboflavin, iron, phosphorus, and potassium and are a very good source for vitamin C, folate, magnesium, and manganese. Add to that the fact that 100 grams of these beans contain only 47 calories, no fat, low sodium, and low carbohydrates, and you'll wonder why you don't eat them every day!

One of my favorite squashes to grow on a fence or other upright support is the Italian heirloom "Trombetta di Albenga," also available from Renee's Garden. (Other seed companies probably sell this squash under a different name, but this is the one I have grown successfully.) The name means "little trumpet from Albenga," and the squash produced is most delicious! (It is not, however, "little.") Nearly seed-free, this relative of zucchini is creamy-colored inside with a smooth, almost artichokey, taste. The outside of the fruit is green, turning to yellow as it gets too ripe. The leaves are big, heart shaped, and beautiful and can even form a nice canopy if you plant on an overhead trellis. This is the best summer squash I have ever tasted, and it is a vigorous plant that grows fast enough to outrun the dread squash vine borer. Although related to zucchini, trombetta is so much tastier and more beautiful that it is hard to find similarities! They are both Italian I guess, but the difference between trombetta and standard zucchini is similar to the difference between canned ravioli and homemade pasta with sauce from fresh tomatoes.

Plant your seeds once the weather is reliably warm. You can put them in the ground or in a large container. Be sure the soil has been enriched with organic material like compost or well-rotted manure, because these plants grow fast and need lots of nutrients. They also need full sun and a steady supply of moisture when they are growing. Mulch well once the plant is several inches tall. Pick the squash when it is 10–12 inches long or smaller. A quick sauté in olive oil with onions and tomatoes makes a wonderful side dish or main course. When the squash is young, the skin is so tender that you don't even need to peel it. As it gets bigger and the weather gets hotter, you might want to peel the outside, but the inside stays firm, moist, and yummy.

Italian heirloom squash "Trombetta" at the farmers' market.

One thing this squash does have in common with regular zucchini is that it is very generous with its fruits. You may find yourself looking for new ways to use the squashes, but you won't want to give it all away. It is too good for that. In addition to simple sautéing, you can add this squash to soup, salad, breads, and any other recipe using summer or winter squash. It is firm enough to hold up during baking and is great when the trumpet is stuffed with a rice and veggie or meat mixture. I have used this squash to make bread-and-butter pickles. Like cucumbers, trombetta squash produces firm, round fruit down to the trumpet end that is perfect for slicing into pickles. When you get to the trumpet, simply cut in half and continue to slice.

BREAD-AND-BUTTER SQUASH PICKLES
16 cups squash, sliced about ¼-inch thick
4 cups onions, thinly sliced (Cut large onions in half before slicing)
½ cup pickling or kosher salt

   4 cups white vinegar
   2 cups granulated sugar
   4 tablespoons whole mustard seed
   2 tablespoons celery seed
   2 teaspoons ground turmeric

Mix squash and onions together in large nonreactive pot and add pickling or kosher salt. Stir to mix.

Add water to cover the vegetables. It is best to use bottled water. Tap water with minerals can discolor your lovely veggies. Cover the pot and let sit for 2 or more hours. Then drain the mixture and rinse out the pot.

Make pickling syrup in the big pot by combining vinegar, sugar, mustard seed, celery see, and ground turmeric. Bring mixture to a boil, stirring to make sure the sugar is well dissolved; then add squash and onions. Mix it well and reduce heat. Simmer 5 minutes.

Fill sterilized pint jars, leaving about ½ inch of headspace, wipe rims, and put on lid. Process in hot-water bath for 10 minutes. Let cool and enjoy or present with great ceremony whenever you need a special gift.

Squash, beans, and peas will all grow happily with the support of a trellis or fence. Melons, on the other hand, need additional support. If you decide to grow honeydews, cantaloupes, small watermelons, or other small melons, you need to help keep the fruit from falling off prematurely. Make a sling with nylon or cotton mesh and secure it underneath the growing melon so that the weight of the melon will be held by the sling rather than the vine. Secure the sling to the fence or trellis. Stockings are perfect for this task. You can also use cheesecloth or other breathable fabric, although you might not want to add bright colors to your vine. Don't use a solid fabric because it will catch moisture and encourage your melon to rot.

A small water-melon rests on mesh plate holder.

Espaliered Trees

If you would like to have a fruit tree in your yard but don't have room for it, consider the old technique known as espalier training. This technique, first developed in the monasteries of Europe, has been adapted by many devoted home gardeners, including George Washington. If you visit Mount Vernon, Washington's home in Virginia, you'll see espaliered apple and fruit trees. Basically, this design turns a three-dimensional tree into a two-dimensional tree and strictly controls its size.

The practice of espaliered fruit trees began in the mid-1600s in France. Monks noticed that fruit growing near the walls of the monastery were less susceptible to freezes and damage in the winter. Father Legendre reasoned that if he planted more trees near the protective walls, he would have more fruit. To avoid overcrowding, he sheared the trees and found that made them more productive.

Espaliered fruit trees today serve several purposes. They are great space savers because they grow right on the fence or wall. They provide easy access to gardeners because the trees remain small, even people with limited mobility can reach the top of the trees, and the branches are less likely to break because they are well controlled. In addition, they are a good choice for a narrow space where bushy plants will take up too much room and limit walking space. Even though the trees are small, they produce a lot of fruit in a limited space.

Espaliered trees are trained to grow in a flat plane against a wall, fence, or trellis. They are not only practical but also highly decorative. You can choose from several patterns to train your tree, but the most common involves a central trunk and three or four tiers of horizontal branches. Another common pattern involves upward-slanting rather than horizontal branches.

The easiest way to begin the project is to decide how you want your tree to look and draw a sketch. If you are using a wall, you can draw your pattern on the wall with chalk or other material; then plant your tree and start snipping and tying. Carefully bend the branches into the desired positions and tie them into place. Remove all unwanted branches. If your design has a central trunk, do not cut the top of the main shoot until the desired height is reached. You can find detailed instructions in other books and online. You can also look at different pattern possibilities and see which appeals most to you. Espalier training involves some fancy pruning and training, but there are many resources available to help you along the way.

To maintain your tree, keep pruning and tying new shoots to maintain the pattern. Remove all stray branches that grow outward or away from the flat surface. Fertilize your young tree with a good organic fertilizer to encourage rapid growth while your pattern is being established. Once it is in place, reduce fertilizer application to once or twice a year.

It is a good idea to plant trees that are growing on dwarfing rootstock. These dwarf trees will naturally remain small and save you a lot of work. Apples are the most common trees for espalier training, but there are other choices as well. You need to select a variety that is well adapted to your location and climate. Good choices for an espalier are apple, loquat, pear, wild plum (Mexican plum and creek plum), Texas persimmon, and Texas mulberry. All of these produce edible fruits and are fairly easy to train into a pattern.

The drawback of espaliering fruit trees is that, if they are grown up against a solid wall or fence, there is poor air circulation, which can encourage disease and pests. Be on the lookout for any potential problem and try to take care of it early. In some cases, simply reducing the amount of foliage and crowding will help. If you are growing on a wire or other openwork fence, this problem is less likely to occur.

Grape Arbors

If you are thinking that a grape arbor might be just the thing in your yard to cover that old porch or gazebo or fence, you may be right. Grapes grow in every part of the United States and all over the world. They like full sun and any type of soil. They produce versatile and sweet fruit and are attractive plants. Why not? The only reason is that you have to prune and train them, and if you don't mind that, then grapes are for you. Talk to someone at a local nursery about the best grapes for your area. Some variety of grape is hardy from USDA zones 2–10, so you want the one that is right for your area. You can choose between table grapes, wine

Grapes growing on an arbor or arch adds interest to a yard and flavor to the table.

grapes, and wild native North American muscadine grapes. Discuss the options with someone who knows, and buy your vines from a local, reputable nursery. You can plant them in the winter or early spring while the plants are dormant. Be sure the support system is in place before you plant. Grapes will happily grow on a chain-link fence or other openwork fencing. Amend the soil or plant your grapes in large containers. (One community garden established on an old tennis court uses raised beds for veggies and half whiskey barrels for grapes around the edges.) Be sure to plant them in an area with plenty of sun and good air circulation. A little afternoon shade won't hurt in most climates. Soak the roots of your new plant in a weak mixture of seaweed and water for a couple of hours before planting. Set the vine into the hole slightly deeper than it was growing in the nursery and water well with the seaweed water.

The vines should not be allowed to produce fruit the first two years so that the root system and canes will mature. Learn about how to prune your particular grapes by looking on the Internet or in a book or contact your local extension service. In just a few years you will have beautiful plants that cover the structure and give you tasty treats. Wild grapes can be made into delicious jellies, jams, and conserves as well as wine. Table grapes, of course, are perfect for eating out of hand, and wine grapes may start you on a whole new career. Growing grapes may take more attention than other edibles, but it is an enjoyable hobby and the grapes are a lovely addition to your landscape and your table.

4   Put It in a Pot, or a Bucket, or a Bag, or...

Almost everyone has a potted plant or two. We grow geraniums in the summer and ivy in the house; we enjoy a flowering amaryllis at Christmastime and African violets on the windowsill. But many of us have not considered growing food in containers.

The advantage of container-grown food is that it can grow almost anywhere! Don't have a yard? Put some plants in containers and grow them on your balcony, porch, or even in a bright window. Hate digging and fighting weeds? Put your edibles in a container and avoid the heavy labor some-times associated with growing plants in the ground. Want some-thing growing on your fence, but your soil is too shallow or poor? Use a container to hold the plant's roots and let the branches soar!

Photo courtesy of Renee's Garden Seeds.

Some people don't think of vegetable, herb, or fruit plants as decorative because they are used to thinking of row crops at the farm. One long row after another of the same plant is sort of boring, but if you look at individual vegetable plants, you'll find that they are indeed lovely. They all grow quickly and have healthy leaves and flowers. Herbs come in all shapes and sizes and are happy to grow in containers. So stop thinking of food as boring and consider it another option for adding beauty and color to your patio, porch, or balcony. Of course, you get to eat it too!

Traditional Containers

The two essentials for growing food in containers are a container of an adequate size and good soil to feed your plants. We've all seen those precious little pots that are sold in stores and catalogs that are labeled "Parsley," "Sage," "Rosemary," and "Thyme." Several springtime "As seen on TV" kits that include tiny pots, herb seeds, and instructions to grow "gourmet gardens" are also to be avoided. The pots are just too small! Herbs are big, healthy, vigorous plants that need room to grow and plenty of sunshine. Attempting to grow them in tiny pots will simply be discouraging, is a waste of money, and leads to inevitable failure. African violets like to grow in tiny pots. Most other plants like room to spread their roots.

You can find large flowerpots at any nursery or big-box store. They are made of plastic, clay, metal, and other materials. You can also buy them at resale shops, garage sales, or recycling centers. Most nurseries will give you used plastic nursery pots that are fine to use again. Use at least 5-gallon pots or larger to grow healthy food plants. You can start your herbs out in 1-gallon pots and move them up to a larger size when they get too big.

Gardeners who have in-ground gardens often find themselves wanting more space in the spring to grow tomatoes, peppers, and other popular plants. Large nursery pots are perfect for that. Even if you grow heirloom varieties of tomatoes that get very tall, you can put them in a big pot. Place a tomato cage inside the pot around the young plants and watch them grow. There are some hybrid tomato varieties designed to grow in containers—"Patio," for example—but any tomato you enjoy eating will grow in a big pot. Don't be swayed by advertising or plant names!

Society garlic grows nicely in containers and is decorative as well.

Speaking of plant names, some tasty and delicious pepper plants that are labeled "ornamental" grow well in pots. Generally, that means that the grower has used chemicals on the plant that make the fruit inedible. Just avoid pepper plants marked "ornamental" altogether. Find a pepper without that warning and enjoy both its flavor and its good looks. Peppers don't mind a bit of shade in the afternoon during the summer, so a partially protected spot would be perfect. Plants can also be fairly small and still produce lots of little peppers. Often they are red, purple, orange, and green all at the same time—tasty and pretty! Some also have purple leaves to add to the color riot.

Calamondin. Photo courtesy of Linda Lehmusvirta.

One class of edibles that includes many plants happy to grow in pots is citrus. Even in cold climates you can grow lemons, tangerines, oranges, and other citrus trees in containers. You simply have to protect them when the weather gets cold. Some varieties will even grow happily indoors if your spot is bright enough—6–8 hours of sunshine or bright light. In warmer climates, many varieties can be left outdoors year-round. Dwarf oranges, particularly satsuma mandarin (*Citrus reticulata*), are recommended for anyone, including folks living in condos and apartments, as a great variety of homegrown citrus fruit. It is a beautiful plant with dark green, glossy foliage and fragrant flowers. The leaves are green year-round, and the flowers generally appear in March or April. The fruit itself is juicy and sweet and almost seedless. It is cold tolerant to the mid-20s. If it gets colder, the plant needs to be moved indoors to someplace where the temperature will remain higher; often a garage will do.

Satsuma oranges are often sold in 5-gallon containers and should be transplanted into larger pots, generally about 15 gallons. Black plastic nursery pots can be obtained either free or inexpensively from nurseries that sell trees. The trees live a long time when they are happy but will not grow too tall for your home. Generally, even after many years in its container, the plant will reach only 4–6 feet tall. Satsuma is not only a lovely plant with tasty fruit, but it is easy to grow. It needs water only when the soil is dry an inch below the surface. You can get a little probe that will tell you or rely on your trusty finger. Don't overwater! Satsuma is a fairly drought-tolerant plant, and you're more likely to kill it by overwatering than by underwatering.

All citrus plants thrive in full sun. They need as much sun as they can get with a minimum of 6 hours per day. They are also all cold sensitive to varying degrees, so find out what your particular plant requires when you buy it. You can grow lemons, limes, grapefruits, tangerines, and

Calamondin. Photo courtesy of Linda Lehmusvirta.

kumquats. Look for dwarf varieties to make sure the plant won't quickly outgrow your pot. Kumquats are naturally small, so a dwarf kumquat isn't always necessary, although there are dwarf varieties.

Kumquats (or cumquats) (*Fortunella margarita*) are less common than some other citrus plants, but they are fun to grow in your container garden. They have been called the "little gems of the citrus family." The fruit are oval shaped with bright golden-yellow to reddish-orange peels. The peels are thin and sweet, and the inside is tart, so the whole fruit is eaten at once for a blend of sweet-tart tastiness. They can also be used to make a delicious marmalade. The plants have pointed, glossy, green leaves that are evergreen, and the flowers are sweetly fragrant, as are most citrus flowers.

Calamondin (*Citrus mitis*) comes from China and was originally called "acid orange" because of its sour flavor. It is widely grown as an ornamental, but it is not only a lovely plant and tolerates lower temperatures than many other citrus species but is also a useful edible fruit. The juice can be used in place of lemon or lime juice to make refreshing drinks, cakes, pies, and marmalades or added to any recipe that calls for lemon or lime. The orange-colored fruit is small, about an inch in diameter. The fruit has few seeds, and the bush is nearly thornless. The calamondin produces lots of fruit that resembles small tangerines, and the tree has beautiful leaves and flowers. The plant can bloom year-round, lending a wonderful fragrance to the patio or balcony where it is growing. It should grow outdoors except in the coldest weather. Flowers and fruit will often appear at the same time, making it particularly ornamental. The flowers are self-fertile, so you need not have multiple plants to be sure of fruit set. If you are anxious for more fruit, you can force the tree to bloom by withholding water until the leaves become wilted and roll up. A thorough watering will then produce a flush of blooms within 2 months.

Fresh calamondins can be halved or quartered and served with iced or hot tea, seafood, or any other dish that will benefit from a quick splash of piquancy. A delicious marmalade can be made by combining equal parts calamondin and kumquat. You can also simply juice the fruit and freeze the juice in ice-cube trays for later use.

MIXED MARMALADE

Equal amounts of calamondins and kumquats, halved and seeded
Water to cover fruit
1 cup sugar to each cup fruit
Juice of lemon

Place halved, seeded fruit in water to cover; cook until skin is soft. Leave fruit in pan, cover, and allow to soak in juices overnight. Measure 1 cup of sugar to each cup of fruit and add the juice of a lemon or as much as you desire for tartness.

Cook at very high heat until the mixture boils. Then begin stirring and cook, stirring constantly for 15 minutes but never more than 20 minutes. If overcooked, the marmalade will be solid and will not spread.

Pour into jars and seal.

CALAMONDIN CAKE ("BEST CAKE IN THE WORLD" FROM COOKS.COM)

1 package lemon supreme cake mix
¾ cup oil
½ cup sugar
4 eggs
¼ cups pureed calamondin, seeds removed
1 cup confectioners' sugar

Preheat oven to 325°F. Mix lemon cake mix, oil, sugar, eggs, and 1 cup calamondin at medium speed for 2 minutes. Pour into a well-greased and floured Bundt pan.

Bake 1 hour. After taking cake from oven, pour a mixture of confectioners' sugar and ¼ cup calamondin over top of hot cake.

All citrus fruits take a long time to mature. Most bloom in late winter or early spring and then ripen throughout the summer and into the fall. It is not uncommon for citrus to begin ripening in November and continue through the winter months. (We always have lemon pie with Thanksgiving dinner.) Half whiskey barrels are about 15 gallons in size and are a good choice of container for growing citrus trees. Nursery pots

Meyer lemons are favorite container fruits.

or ornamental pots of the same size are also fine. Just be sure your pot provides drainage at the bottom. Select a potting mixture that is designed for container growing. It should drain easily and contain nutrients in the form of compost. You can grow annuals around your citrus tree in a large pot, adding interest and flavor in some cases. Select edible flowers or low-growing herbs to maximize the harvest from your big container. Once the tree grows large enough to fill the pot with roots, there won't be room for the flowers. Water thoroughly when the soil is dry. Make sure the water is not running down the inside of the pot and not soaking into the root ball. Let the soil dry out before thoroughly watering again. You will have to water more often in the heat of summer and less often in winter. Use organic fertilizer designed for citrus trees if you can find it or use one for fruit trees with micronutrients included. Give your tree a boost with a monthly addition of seaweed when you water. When the temperature gets to about 30°F, move your tree to a protected area where temperatures will not drop too low.

A strawberry pot is a traditional-style terra-cotta pot that many people overlook. Strawberry pots come in a variety of sizes from fairly small to really big. They come glazed or unglazed, decorated or plain. Designed to grow several strawberry plants at one time, these are a clever idea that actually works. It is wise to avoid the little bitty cute pots because they don't have room for roots. Select a good-sized strawberry pot, either new or used. Get a piece of PVC pipe and drill holes in it. Cut the pipe to a length just a little taller than the height of your pot and secure it in the center. You will water through the top of this pipe, and as the water filters out the holes you drilled, the soil will not be washed away. You can use one pipe or three smaller ones tied together with string. Whatever you have on hand or can easily acquire works. Put the pipe in the pot

Strawberry pots can be found both new and vintage.

Photo courtesy of Renee's Garden Seeds.

and then add soil at the bottom of the pot. When you come to a hole, put your little strawberry plant in from the inside if possible. Add soil to anchor the plant and repeat the process as you move upward. Top off the pot with soil, but be sure the pipe stands a little bit above the surface for easy watering.

Use a water-soluble fertilizer to keep your plants growing vigorously and be sure to water through the pipe. You'll be surprised at how many delicious strawberries will grow in your pot. This is a great project for kids. Everything is just the right size for small hands. And they will love finding the berries and eating them. Probably few berries will make it into the house, but that's okay too.

Another group of edible plants that are naturals for container grow-ing are greens. Lettuce, chard, spinach, oriental greens, and more grow in cool temperatures, when they don't need a lot of soil to keep their roots from getting too hot. They also grow into compact plants that neatly fit into flowerpots and other containers. Start with seeds or transplants in small pots and move up gradually as the plants grow. You can combine different colors and varieties of lettuce in a big pot to have a lovely, as well as tasty, addition to your porch or yard. Greens can stand afternoon shade but need good morning light.

Nontraditional Containers

For years we grew Swiss chard in a wheelbarrow. We had a fairly shady lawn, so we moved the wheelbarrow around, chasing the sunlight. Chard is one of the few greens that will pretty much grow year-round even in hot climates. (Chard also looks great in your flower beds if you have room there.)

Swiss chard is a member of the common beet family, which is too often overlooked or ignored when planning a garden. Rich in vitamin C, calcium, and iron, chard is not the imported, delicate, gourmet vegetable that its name implies. Chard grows easily in almost every soil, is impervious to both hot and cold weather, and tastes delicious. The plant does not form an edible root as beets do, but it does put down deep, fibrous roots that are helpful in aerating and loosening the soil. More important, however, chard is dependable and very versatile in the kitchen.

There are two basic types of chard. The kind with large center stems and big leaves is called Swiss chard or stem chard. Smaller leaves with insignificant stems are known as perpetual spinach or leaf beets. Both types bear through hot and cool weather in most every section of the country. There are a variety of choices of chard that will give you beautiful plants—the center stems can be green or white, but they can also be red, orange, or yellow. A mixture of colors makes for a great-looking planting wherever they are located.

Harvest single leaves from the outside of the plants as they grow, and new leaves will appear in the center. Chard is much more tolerant of heat than most salad and cooking greens. Spinach and lettuces usually bolt as soon as the weather becomes dependably warm, but chard continues to grow and produce even when hot weather arrives. In USDA zones 8–10, chard can be grown year-round in the garden, and in cooler areas, it lasts a long time. You can also extend the season by mulching deeply with straw or other material when frosts begin or hauling (or rolling) your container inside on cold nights.

Mostly pest-free, chard leaves are occasionally munched on by passing marauders, but generally you need not worry about insects on this sturdy plant. It needs good soil, but no special fertilizing, and is fairly drought resistant, although it appreciates regular, deep watering.

Young, tender leaves can be eaten raw in salads. Chard is a favorite vegetable to add to stir-fries because it adds both the crunch of the stem and the substance of the leaves. When leaves become larger and weather hotter, sometimes it is best to cook the leaves, but they remain delicious. The sturdy center stems can be cooked with the leaves as you would spinach, or they can be removed and cooked separately as if they were asparagus or chopped and eaten raw as you would celery. Sauté chard, add to soups, or use as a substitute for spinach in many recipes.

SWISS CHARD AND RICE

½ cup onion, chopped
1 clove garlic, minced
4 tablespoons butter
1 pound Swiss chard, shredded (remove stems)
1 cup raw white rice
3 cups hot chicken stock
Salt and pepper to taste
Romano or Parmesan cheese, grated

In a large skillet with a lid, sauté the onion and garlic in butter until light golden-brown. Add the chard and sauté until limp. Add the rice and evenly distribute with the chard in the pan. Pour in the hot stock and season with salt and pepper. Cover and simmer 20 minutes or until the rice is cooked. Sprinkle with grated cheese and serve immediately. This is an excellent main course or side dish.

SWISS CHARD QUICHE

½ pound fresh chard, stemmed and washed (chop leaves coarsely and slice stems, keep separate)
¼ cup onion, minced
¼ cup chard stems, sliced
1 tablespoon butter or oil
3 large eggs
1 scant cup milk

¼ teaspoon salt

Dash of ground pepper

Dash of Worcestershire sauce

1 cup Monterey Jack cheese, grated

¼ cup Parmesan cheese, grated

1 pie crust

Preheat oven to 350°F. Blanch the chard leaves, drain, and run under cold water. Squeeze out the liquid by twisting chard in a towel. Chop fine. Sauté the onion and chard stems in the butter or oil until crisp-tender. Beat the eggs and blend with the milk; then beat in the salt, pepper, and Worcestershire sauce.

In a large bowl, toss together the onion and stems, blanched chard, and the cheeses. Spread half the mixture over the bottom of the pie shell. Pour in the egg-milk mixture and top with the remaining cheese mixture.

Bake 30–40 minutes until firm to the touch. Let cool a few minutes before serving.

CHARD-STUFFED TOMATOES

1 pound fresh chard, stemmed and chopped, reserve stems for
  another dish

6 firm-ripe tomatoes

1 tablespoon green onion, chopped

½ teaspoon garlic salt

¼ teaspoon dried or 1 teaspoon fresh oregano

1 teaspoon fresh lemon juice

Cook chard in only the liquid that clings to the leaves after it has been washed. Cook in a covered pot on high heat until it begins to steam, then reduce heat immediately, and cook about 2 minutes. Remove from heat and let drain. Chop fine.

Remove pulp from tomatoes (reserve the shells) and combine drained chard, tomato pulp, onion, garlic salt, oregano, and lemon juice. Spoon vegetable mixture into tomato shells.

These may be served cold as a salad on crisp greens or placed in a glass pie plate and baked in a 350°F oven for 15 minutes until heated through.

Students at Connally High School in Austin grow food gardens in galvanized tin containers.

Speaking of wheelbarrows and such, there are many options for planting besides flowerpots. Wheelbarrows are just one choice. You can use galvanized tin containers in every shape and size. Look at any yard sale or thrift store, and you are likely to find old tin tubs with rusted-out holes in the bottom. There are big tubs and little tubs, round tubs and oval tubs. Any and all of these make good planters. As long as the whole bottom isn't rusted away, the pots are great containers for planting veggies and flowers.

Other metal containers that are easy to find and recycle into plant containers are old porcelain cook pots and wash pots. These come in white, blue, green, and speckled with red trim and other combinations. You can stick to red and white, for example, or mix it up with a variety of colors. Grouped together, these items from days gone by are once again useful and good-looking tools.

When you are planning your container kitchen garden, let your imagination take flight. To have an interesting and beautiful container garden, look around at other options and consider unlikely places to find great containers. First, think of traditional garden containers out of their usual context. Use hanging baskets for trailing plants like strawberries, cherry tomatoes, oregano, and thyme instead of petunias and phlox. Lettuce also does well in hanging baskets, and you can place it near the doorway so fresh salad is always handy. Strawberries do well in a strawberry pot, but also try using a strawberry pot as a multistoried herb garden, placing different herbs into each of the little holes. A large strawberry pot will provide ample space for root growth even though the openings where the plants emerge are small.

Half whiskey barrels are good for plants that need larger root space— tomatoes, dwarf fruit trees, even a collection of root plants like onion, carrots, and beets. An old porcelain washing machine or a child's plastic swimming pool can host miniature gardens that have a unique and interesting look.

Teakettles, top hats, worn-out cowboy boots—if it will hold soil, it can be a planter. Even the nurseries are offering some untraditional planting containers. A British company, Haxnicks, makes planting containers in a variety of sizes from tough polyethylene with reinforced drainage

Bags can be purchased ready to fill with soil and plants.

holes. Especially designed for use on patios, on balconies, and in small gardens, the vegetable planters range from shopping-bag size up to kiddie–swimming pool size. The smaller bags have handles on each side for easy carrying and can be folded flat for storage when not in use. They are reasonably priced and easy to use. Whatever container you decide to use must have holes in the bottom for drainage. If your container holds quite a bit of soil, you might want to add a layer of gravel, Styrofoam peanuts, or wood chips in the bottom to improve drainage and requires less potting soil. If there are no holes or not enough holes, you can add some. The filler in the bottom will help keep the soil from plugging up the drainage holes.

The key to container gardening, however, is not the container but the soil. Plants in the ground can send their roots out searching for nutrients and moisture. Plants in containers are limited by the size of the container. So the key to success is using a soil mix rich in nutrients and continuing to replenish the nutrients as they are used up or washed away. Begin with a good potting soil that contains compost. You can also plant directly in well-aged compost. The soil should be light so it does not compact and air can get to the roots.

Remember that containers dry out and lose nutrients faster than soil in the ground. You'll need to water your containers more often than you would garden beds. Every time you water, you are washing nutrients out of the soil. Establish a regular feeding schedule—give your plants a foliar feeding of fish emulsion and seaweed every 2 weeks or so. Add a thin layer of compost to the top of the pot once a month.

Be sure to keep picking the fruit as it ripens to keep the plants producing. Place your containers in a sunny spot. Almost all vegetables need full sun. Once you have your fresh veggies growing in your containers, you can sit back with a cool glass of herb tea and enjoy the bounty of the harvest.

There are many food plants, such as the following, that can be grown in containers:

Dwarf fruit trees: apple, cherries, figs, pears
Berries
Citrus trees

Eggplant growing in containers. Photo courtesy of Renee's Garden Seeds.

Pineapple

Tomatoes, peppers, squash, cucumbers, cantaloupe, small water melon, and eggplant

Almost any herb will be happy in a container: basil, oregano, parsley, rosemary, chives, catnip, thyme, sage, parsley, bay leaf

Leafy greens: kale, mesclun, spinach, lettuce, mustard, collard, arugula, chard

Root vegetables need a deeper container than other crops: carrots, beets, potatoes, turnips

5   Food Just Grows on Trees

Almost every yard has a tree or two. Did you ever think that those trees could be providing not only shade but also food? Now you probably don't want to go chop down your oak tree, but the next time you want to add a tree to your landscape, consider one that does double duty.

Many years ago when we moved from the city to the country, my husband had his first experience with pecan trees. There were several big old trees in our new yard, and he was amazed. "Food just falls from the sky!" he exclaimed, more than once. It is true. Nut trees and fruit trees are good looking, add value to your home, provide shade and a place to sit and play, and give you great things to eat.

Bailey, sweet girl with sweet peaches!

Growing a food-giving tree is a much longer-term project than planting a tomato. You need to select your tree carefully, plant it well, and care for it as it grows. The kind of tree you plant will depend on what grows best in your area. The best way to decide is to talk to local nursery people and your local extension service. Those people know what grows best in their location and can advise you on varieties and types of trees to choose. Although those trees that you used to see in the Sunday supplement with branches bearing peaches, plums, pears, and avocados and roots with potatoes on them look good, it is highly unlikely that they will grow in your (or any) yard. Fruit trees, in particular, are susceptible to temperature, soil, and other climate considerations. It isn't that they are especially hard to grow; you just have to grow the right ones. The same is true of nut trees, and in addition they are often very large and need lots of space.

Fruit

No matter how much you love fresh sour cherries baked into a pie, if you live in the warm South, you can't grow those cherry trees. They like the cold; they need the cold; they can't live without the cold. And they can't take the heat. On the other hand, people in Wisconsin who grow fabulous sour cherries will fail miserably at growing peaches. While peaches will grow in USDA zones 5–9, they do best in zones 6–7. Georgia peaches, Texas peaches, Arkansas peaches—these are the ones people talk about and brag about. If you want to grow peaches (or any other fruit), inquire locally and find out which varieties are best adapted to your location.

In addition to finding out what climate fruit trees require, you will need to know how many you have to plant. Some fruit trees need another tree to ensure pollination and production of fruit. If you have limited space, look for self-pollinating varieties that will allow you to plant only one tree and still get fruit.

The other consideration is size. How much room do you have, and how big is the fruit tree of your dreams going to get? The good news is that many fruit trees have been hybridized so that dwarf varieties are readily available. These trees are programmed to grow smaller in size but produce standard-sized fruit. Dwarf and semi-dwarf trees also have the advantage of being closer to the ground when it comes time to prune and harvest the tree. Dwarf trees are also great for espalier training. (See the previous chapter for details.)

Once you select your tree, take some time to decide on the best place to plant it. Too many trees are planted too close to a structure, which causes problems for the tree and the structure. Find out how big the tree will be when it is fully grown and allow for that space around it. It is hard to imagine that the tiny stick you buy at the nursery with turn into something 30 feet tall and 50 feet wide, but it may. Plant your tree so it has plenty of room to expand. Also plant it with regard to how you want it to function in your landscape. If you need protection from the north wind, plant your tree on the north side of the house. If you want shade in the afternoon, select a site in the west. Smaller, understory trees can be planted close to big trees, but you need to give big trees plenty of room to grow.

The old saying about a fifty-dollar hole and a ten-dollar plant holds true of trees as well as other plants. Do a good job digging your hole. It is going to serve as the home base for your tree for years to come. Dig a square hole but don't smooth out the sides of the hole. Leave them rough. You don't want to create a container in the ground but rather a place from which the roots can expand and reach out. Dig the hole much larger than the root ball of your tree. Pile the dirt you remove from the hole outside the hole and mix that soil with about a third as much compost. Backfill the hole with that mixture once your tree has been planted. If the dirt in the hole is too rich, it will discourage the roots from leaving the hole and they will end up going around and around in a circle. You want to feed them, but you also want them to be accustomed to the native soil in which they are supposed to grow. Some experts recommend using only the native soil to backfill the hole. You can add compost or not, but if you decide to add some, be stingy with it.

Once the tree is planted, water it well and cover the top of the soil with a good layer of mulch. Mixing a water-soluble fertilizer such as a seaweed-fish emulsion blend will help get it off to a good start, and mulching with compost is always a boon. Remember to plant your young tree at the level it was growing or slightly above. Roots can turn into bark, but bark cannot turn into roots, and burying the bark is dangerous to the

"Methley" plum tree loaded with fruit.

tree. When you put down your mulch, be sure it does not pile up against the trunk of the tree. Keep it a small distance from the trunk and then extend it to edge of the planting hole of a new tree or the drip line of an established tree.

New trees require more water than established trees. Be sure to water when the soil gets dry around the tree. Mulch will help keep the moisture in and also keep weeds from growing around the base of the tree. Using a compost or mulch that contains mycorrhizae fungus will help encourage the new roots growing on your tree. A feeding of seaweed every two weeks or so will also help those baby roots spread out and grow and discourage transplant shock from hurting your new tree. You will need to add supplementary water to your tree at least for a year unless you have plenty of rain. It takes that long for the feeder roots to become established.

You won't need to fertilize a new tree the first year. Established trees, however, will benefit from an annual feeding of organic fertilizer and a good mulching with compost. This extra food helps keep the tree healthy and more able to withstand pest and disease attacks. Keep in mind that any grass or flowers growing beneath the tree are competing for moisture and nutrients, so be sure there is plenty for everyone!

Once your tree is well established, it should require little care, but don't ignore your mature trees entirely. Monitor them regularly for insects and signs of disease. Many trees are kept healthy by the presence of beneficial insects in their canopy. Releasing beneficial wasps and ladybugs will help control worms and aphids that can attack the leaves. A spraying with Bt (*Bacillus thuringiensis*) will take care of a heavy infestation of any kind of caterpillar and will not hurt any of the beneficials around. Regular feeding, mulching, and watering during very dry spells will help keep your trees healthy and your landscape beautiful.

Plums are the poster child of yummy fruit. Just consider how we use the word: "plum job," "plum assignment," and "plum (meaning completely) pretty." The Cambridge dictionary lists the second definition as "something that is very good and worth having." The first definition, of course, is "a small round fruit with a smooth skin, sweet flesh and single large seed." We want both in our yards—fruit and very good.

In addition to producing tasty fruit, plum trees make nice, smallish shade trees, and the flowers that bloom in the spring are beautiful and fragrant. Generally white, the blossoms cover the branches and give off a wonderful scent as long as they are in bloom. It is worth the sacrifice to bring a blooming stem indoors to enjoy the perfume.

There are three different types of plum trees that grow in the United States. Japanese types (*Prunus salicina*) date back centuries, and you can see their flowers on ancient oriental artwork. In the United States, Japanese plums such as "Santa Rosa" and "Burbank" were bred by Luther Burbank. Japanese plums bud and bloom earlier than other varieties, making them a good choice for zones 5 and warmer. The fruit of Japanese plum trees is delicious for eating fresh. Most of the plums you find in the grocery store come from this type of tree. When you plant Japanese plums in your garden, you will often need to plant two different varieties to ensure pollination. Japanese plums thrive in warmer areas where peach trees also thrive. One great choice is "Methley," which is self-pollinating and hardy in zones 5–9. It bears lots of reddish-purple fruit with sweet, juicy, red flesh.

European plums (*P. domestica*) are smaller and more likely to be self-fertile than Japanese fruit. Several prune plums are the European type, as well as "Green Gage," a green tangy fruit, and "Mirabells," a yellow fruit. "Stanley" is a versatile European plum that is well suited to the eastern and northwestern regions of the United States. European types are more cold tolerant than Japanese types and take longer to mature.

The third type of plum tree available commercially in the United States is the American hybrid. It can be Japanese-American or European-American but has the distinction of being developed in the United States for specific conditions. These trees, a.k.a. "bush plums," will produce well in cold weather and as far south as Florida. They are inclined to be bushier, hence the common name, and produce sweet and tasty fruit. There is also a beach plum that grows from Maine to Delaware and is tolerant of sea spray and sand.

One of the parents of the American hybrid is the American plum (*P. americana*). This group contains several native plum trees that produce fruit that varies in size and taste. Native plums are usually shrubby and often form thickets. The fruit is particularly appealing to wildlife, and many people plant these trees for just that reason. The fruit, often small and tangy, makes great jelly. The native trees are hardy to zone 3 and are even drought tolerant. Some cultivated varieties are available, and you can grow these natives from seed gathered from wild trees in your area.

So, how do you know which plum to plant? As always, ask around. European plum trees are adapted to most areas of the United States. They can take more cold, but Japanese varieties can take more heat. American hybrids have been developed to do well in specific local conditions. For example, some survive in northern plains where there is unbroken, persistent cold, while other varieties do well in regions where cold and warmth are intermittent in the winter. Thus, it is important to check with a knowledgeable local fruit grower or seller. A plum is not a plum is not a plum. You have to get the right plum to be happy with your tree and the fruit it produces.

Figs produce generously.

One of the easiest fruit trees to grow is the fig. Fig trees will grow unprotected in zones 8–10 and in colder areas if you choose hardy varieties and give them some winter protection. There are more than two hundred kinds of figs that grow in North America, so it is essential that you inquire locally to find the best one for your garden. "Brown Turkey," "Celeste," and "Chicago" are good choices for colder climates. These will also grow well in warmer areas, as will "Kadota," which is grow commercially in California. It is particularly important to try to buy fruit trees from a reputable local nursery that knows the area. North of zone 6, figs should not be planted in the ground but grown in containers or greenhouses instead.

The fig is one of the oldest fruit crops around. You can read about figs in the Bible and other historical sources, and they have been an important home fruit crop in the South for more than a century. Be sure that the tree you buy is self-pollinating. The ones that are not rely on a tiny wasp native to the Mediterranean area for pollination. That critter might be hard to find in your neighborhood!

Once you have selected your fig tree, all you have to do is find a spot in full sun and away from buildings where it can grow. Figs get wider than tall, so expect your tree to spread out. Try to find a spot where the tree will be protected from strong winter winds. Plant it in well-drained soil and mulch with compost to get it off to a good start. Figs are adaptable plants that grow well in containers or espaliered on a fence. Water and feed regularly to keep them growing well, but otherwise these trees are good at taking care of themselves. The major annoyance with fig trees is that birds love the ripe fruit almost as much as people do. You can try various techniques to scare off the birds—CDs tied in the branches to flash in the wind, white cloths to do the same, netting, or sporadic noise or water devices. The birds will still get a few, but usually you will still have plenty to enjoy. My mother, who loved figs, tied aluminum pie pans and white rags in the tree to scare away the birds. She always said the birds used the pans as plates and the rags as napkins.

The American persimmon (*Diospyros virginiana*), also known as the common persimmon, is native from Florida to Connecticut, west to Iowa, and south to Texas. Persimmon trees grow in USDA zones 4–9. The persimmon is a rather small tree that fits well into home landscapes, but it does require both a male and female tree in the area to produce fruit. The Asian persimmon is an import that is also well adapted to most parts of the country. The Asian varieties are self-fertile, so you need only one tree to produce fruit. Whichever variety you choose, the persimmon is a beautiful tree with tasty fruit at just the time of year you are wishing for tasty fruit.

The American persimmon grows wild in many areas where small groves are found in abandoned pastures and along fence rows. The fruit

Persimmon tree full of fruit.

is famous for its astringency (makes your mouth pucker!) and can't be eaten until after the first frost and when all the leaves have fallen from the tree. The Texas persimmon (*D. texana*) has a small purple fruit and is best known for its peeling bark that reveals white, gray, and pink on the trunk beneath. The Asian persimmon (*D. kaki*) came to the United States in the late 1800s from China and Japan. The American persimmon serves as an excellent rootstock for propagating Asian varieties.

Persimmon trees have taproots that grow deep into the ground, so they are usually able to find water even during droughts. When you plant your tree, dig a deep hole to encourage the roots. Add a little compost to the native soil and fill the hole with the mixture. Keep the new tree well watered until it is established. After that, persimmon trees need little care. They don't generally need fertilizing unless they appear to be stressed. Pests rarely bother persimmon trees. As is the case for all trees, it is good to have a layer of mulch under the tree to cut down on competition from grass and weeds for nutrients and water.

The fruit of the persimmon stays on the tree once the leaves have fallen and the weather has dropped below freezing. The result is a beautiful tree that looks as though it has been decorated for Christmas with shiny bright balls hanging from the branches. The fruit must be fully ripe and soft before being eaten. Frost does not cause ripening, just usually accompanies it. When the astringent varieties are soft to the touch, they are generally ripe and sweet. Nonastringent varieties can be eaten as soon as they develop a deep, rich, orange color. Read about the variety you choose to learn how to recognize ripeness. Persimmons ripen off the tree as well as on the branches. You can store the fruit on the tree for a long time provided there are not any critters coming to eat it. The fruit has sweet, jellylike flesh generally eaten fresh. It can also be dried. Persimmons contain more vitamin C than citrus and contain an abundance of other nutrients.

If you live in a warm climate, you might enjoy planting some olive trees. For some time people believed that olives grew only in the Mediterranean region, but we've learned that they can thrive in other climates. Olive trees have been around for a very long time. Written records dating back to 3000 BC tell of trees growing in Syria. Franciscan

Persimmons are ripe when they are very soft.

Olives in South Texas.
Photo courtesy of Sandy
Oaks Olive Orchard.

friars brought the trees to California in the 1700s when they established missions there, and the trees have continued to grow and produce there since. During the 1980s there was a renewed interest in growing olives in the United States, and experiments started in various states.

Most American olives are still grown in California, but there are now producing trees in New Mexico, Texas, and Arizona. Olives like warm, dry climates, although some varieties are hardy down to 15°F for short periods. Areas where temperatures swing quickly between hot and cold cause particular difficulty for olive growers. Still, producing olives and olive oil can be an adventure for home gardeners. All parts of the olive tree are useful. The wood is highly prized for creating carvings, bowls, and other decorative objects. The leaves make a tea that is powerful in antioxidants, vitamin C, and other nutritional boosters. The fruit and oil are tasty in a variety of uses.

If you want to grow one or two olive trees in your garden, visit an olive grower and learn about the different varieties and their requirements. Many varieties are self-fertile, so you don't need to worry about having multiple trees to ensure fruit production. Some are more cold hardy than others. Olive trees need a long, hot summer and a cool, but not frigid, winter to thrive. Because olive trees stay relatively small, they are easy to add to existing landscapes. They should be situated so that they have protection from cold north winds if possible. They need full sun and the best drainage possible. They were traditionally planted in areas where the soil was not good enough for other crops—sandy, rocky hillsides with poor soil and places where water was scarce. Many trees are planted on a hill, either natural or created, to make sure that water drains away from the tree trunk. Olive trees are shallow-rooted plants. Don't plant them too deep or overplant them with other greenery. The roots need to be near the surface for the tree to live a long time and produce well.

In addition to making fruit and oil, olive trees are lovely to look at. The slender, grayish leaves will be an evergreen cooling feature in your yard. The breeze blowing through the branches makes a delightful sound. If you aren't familiar with olive trees, visit a commercial grower in your area to decide if this tree is right for you. In the event of short cold spells, you can protect your trees by festooning them with Christmas lights or throwing a blanket over them. The small size of the trees makes them easier to protect than other trees.

Even in cooler climates, it is possible to grow olive trees in large containers. The tree needs to be planted in a big pot with ample drainage holes and set on blocks to make sure the holes are able to drain. Good potting soil that drains well will be fine for planting your tree. It will need to be watered when the soil feels dry to the touch and should be fertilized in the spring and again in midsummer. Put your pot in full sun. If you need to bring it in for frost protection, return it to the sunshine as soon as temperatures rise. You can snip back the ends of the branches to encourage bushiness, and when the roots appear to be filling the pot, take the plant out and trim back the roots to allow for more fresh soil.

While your home olive tree may not produce well enough to supply your family with oil for the year, you can enjoy tea from the leaves and brined green olives on your table. Olives fresh from the tree are pretty bitter and unpleasant tasting. They need brining before they become the treats we know and love. Here is the method suggested by Sandy Oaks Olive Orchard just south of San Antonio.

BRINING OLIVES

Select only olives without flaws. To paraphrase an old adage: One spoiled olive ruins the batch. Make a solution of 1½ cups sea salt or kosher salt (without iodine) mixed in 1 gallon of water. Place the olives in a glass or ceramic container and cover with the salt and water mixture. Keep the olives from floating by weighing down with a gallon plastic sealable bag filled with water. Be sure they are submerged in the brine. Store in a cool place—about 64°F–72°F is ideal.

In about 6 weeks, taste an olive. If it is tasty, start using them. If it is still bitter, continue the process. If they seem too salty, pour off brine and soak in cool water for several hours. Drain and cover with fresh water. Store in the refrigerator and enjoy.

Nuts

Like fruit trees, the kinds of nut trees that you can add to your landscape depend on where you live. Almonds, chestnuts, hazelnuts, hickory, pine nuts, pecans, pistachios, and walnuts all grow in various parts of the United States, but there are few, if any, places where all of them will grow. All nuts are highly nutritious, containing significant amounts of protein. Some nuts grow on large shade-providing trees that take several years before they start producing. Others grow on bushes that can double as shrubs and will produce in only a few years. Whether you are planting and planning for the seventh generation or for a few years down the road, the addition of nuts to your garden is a great idea. All nut trees (and fruit trees and other trees) should be planted when they are dormant in late winter or very early spring. All of them need full sun, and the better the soil, the better the tree will be. Trees should be planted in native soil slightly amended so they are prepared to grow as quickly as possible.

Almond (Prunus spp.) Almond trees are attractive and grow 15–30 feet tall. They have the same requirements as peach trees, but there are not as many varieties available. Like peaches, almonds require a period of chilling during the winter. The problem with almond trees is that they are apt to bloom at the first sign of warm weather in late winter, and the crop is often lost with the next hard frost.

Tree nuts, including almonds, walnuts, pine nuts, and pecans, all taste good and are packed with nutrition.

If you live in a warm region and want to take a chance, almonds generally produce fruit in about 3 years. The trees bloom with a profusion of white flowers, and the nut is part of the seed of the fruit that the tree produces. Since it is a relative of peaches and plums, the seeds look similar. There are sweet and bitter almonds. The bitter almond is not edible and contains cyanide. Sweet almonds are the type offered by nurseries to home gardeners. Check with local gardeners or your extension service to see if almonds have a chance of survival in your area.

Chestnut (Castanea spp.) Chestnut trees were once prevalent in US forests but were attacked in the last century by chestnut blight, and most trees were wiped out. Some survivors were found, however, and from those, new hybrids have been developed. Chinese chestnuts were also imported and are resistant to the blight. Like pecan and walnut, chestnut trees are large, distinguished-looking trees that can take several years to grow to maturity. Chestnuts are the fastest growing of these big trees and can begin to produce fruit as early as 4 years after they are planted. You must have room for these trees since they can grow up to and sometimes beyond 50 feet tall with wide canopies. Chestnuts are hardy in zones 4–8 and do best when there are two others nearby to ensure pollination and nut production. Chestnut trees are very cold hardy and do best in areas where forests are naturally occurring. Chestnuts require well-drained soil and do not tolerate very heavy clay or limestone soils.

Hazelnut (Corylus spp.) Hazelnuts are also known as filberts and often appear in mixed-nut bowls during the winter holidays. They grow on large shrubs that reach 6–10 feet tall and wide. They are hardy in zones 4–8. The nuts are produced 3 years after planting, and the foliage turns a brilliant orange-red in the fall. It is best to plant two varieties to ensure pollination.

Hazelnuts naturally appear at the edge of a forest, so they prefer dappled shade and soil that is well drained. American hazelnuts are very cold hardy. They are native in areas from Maine to Oklahoma. There were once large thickets of hazelnut bushes in the United States, but they have fallen to land clearers. They don't like hot summers, so they are not good choices for Texas, New Mexico, and other hot areas. Most hazelnuts are grown in Oregon.

Hickory (Carya spp.) Hickory nuts grow on several varieties of hickory trees, which are large and slow growing. They produce beautiful shade trees and prefer life in a mixed-wood forest. They are both very cold and heat tolerant. They do not tolerate damp soil. Central Texas is about as far west as hickory trees grow, and most grow in eastern forests and rich, well-drained bottomlands. The flavor of the nut is dependent on the variety of the tree. All hickory nuts have a certain bitterness, but many people like that. The bitternut hickory nuts are too bitter to enjoy. The wood of hickory is often used to smoke meat and add delicious flavor to barbecues.

Pecan (Carya spp.) Pecans grow in zones 5–9, which covers a large part of the country. Some varieties are adapted to specific regions, such as the Southeast, North, or Texas. The many varieties of pecan trees produce many kinds of nuts. Just look at the selection of improved pecan nuts—long and short, round and oval, dark-colored and light shells, and even the tiny native pecans that many claim are the most tasty.

The pecan is the state tree of Texas, but this nutritious and delicious nut grows throughout the South, Southwest, and beyond. Pecans are native American trees and were enjoyed by Native American people and later by early settlers. Today the United States produces 85–95 percent of the world's pecans. Pecans are long-lived, large trees. Trees more than 300 years old still produce edible nuts. Since they live so long, they are not fast growers. Some pecan trees begin producing at about 5 years old; others may take longer depending on the variety and where they are growing. It takes a while to establish these large trees, but it is worth the effort if you have room. Just think of how many generations will enjoy the nuts of your labor!

Ask your local nursery person which variety works best in your region. Plant your trees about 50 feet from other trees or from buildings. You should also look up when you plant and make sure your trees will not grow into power lines. Both bare-root and container trees are available. Always buy from a local or nearby source.

Pine nuts (Pinus spp.) Pine nuts, as their name clearly states, come from pine trees. An important common species of pine nut is the seed of *P. pinea.* You can grow these trees from fresh nuts (not the kind you buy at the grocery store) or from seedlings. Look locally and online. It takes about 10 years for an American pine nut tree to start producing cones. These pine trees enjoy desert conditions and grow best in New Mexico and Nevada. They can stand drought and thrive in zones 7–9. The Korean import (*P. koraiensis*) is hardy in zones 4–7 and more tolerant of clay soil.

Pistachio (Pistacia spp.) Pistachio nuts grow and produce best where the climate is arid semi-desert with long, dry, hot summers; low humidity; and cool but not frigid winters, such as California, Arizona, New Mexico, and West Texas. They are pollinated by the wind so they have to be planted where there are frequent mild spring winds. If you can grow pistachios, they make excellent shade trees in addition to the tasty nuts they provide. They grow 25–30 feet tall and are hardy in zones 8–10 where the weather is dry. Both male and female trees are needed for successful nut production.

Walnut (Juglans spp.) Another group of very large trees, walnuts are generally available in black and English varieties. The black walnuts are hardy to zone 4 and reach up to 100 feet in height. They are slow growing and slow in producing nuts, sometimes taking 10 years or so to start producing. The wood has been a favorite of furniture makers for centuries. English walnuts (a.k.a. Persian walnuts and Carpathian walnuts) grow only to about 50 feet tall and will produce nuts in as few as 4 years. They are also hardy to zone 4 and grow all over the United States. Again, check local resources to find out if walnut trees will grow in your yard.

6   Free Foods: Stalking the Wild Whatever

Foraging has been around since the time of our forebears, the hunters and gatherers. Finding food in the wild is an enjoyable way to supplement your diet, get some exercise, and let nature do the major work for you. Every area has native plants that provide edible food for the picking. The trick is finding out what and where they are.

Foraging for Fun and Flavor

If you don't have room for a walnut or pecan tree in your yard, there is a good chance that you can still enjoy the taste and nutrition of fresh nuts and all for free. In areas where they grow well, nut trees are often all around us. They are planted in parks, around public buildings, in woods where there are hiking and biking trails, and along public roads and streets. Squirrels are apt to plant native pecan trees just about anywhere. If the trees are growing on public land, those nuts (as Woody Guthrie would say) belong to you and me.

There are also many people foolish enough to ignore this bounty in their own yards, and they will often be happy to let you pick up the nuts and enjoy them. Most nuts ripen and fall from the trees in the autumn. Be on the lookout for them as you walk around your neighborhood or hike through the woods.

Hickory trees are native to parts of the United States, including the Midwest and most areas of eastern North America and, although not widely grown commercially, produce delicious edible kernels. Foraging for hickory nuts in early autumn is a fun outdoor activity for adventurers of all ages. Locate the trees in your area before the nuts start to fall and then watch. When the nuts begin to fall, usually in early autumn when

Pecan (and other food) trees grow along city streets, in parks, and in other public spaces.

rain or frost loosens them from the tree, get busy. You'll have competition from squirrels, who are skillful nut pickers. Most of the nuts you find will be encased in their rough, dried hulls that have to be removed before shelling. These husks make good mulch for your garden, so take the whole thing home to get ready to eat. Cracking the nuts isn't easy and usually involves a hammer. Practice finding the sweet spot where one blow will fracture along clean lines and reveal the inner kernel. Hickory nuts are rich in oil and buttery in flavor. They can be eaten raw, toasted, or added to recipes. To roast your nuts, put them in a shallow pan and leave them in a 200°F oven until they are golden colored.

Pecan trees have been popular in cities for a long time. You don't have to go foraging in the woods to find them in areas where they grow. Pecans grow on street corners, in parks, and in yards, and in most years tons of these delicious nuts go to waste because nobody picks them up. Pecans contain more than nineteen vitamins and minerals, very few carbohydrates, and no cholesterol and are a source of high-quality protein. Research shows that pecans are helpful in maintaining a healthy heart and are high in antioxidants that protect overall good health.

Pecans generally start falling from their trees in October or November, depending on the weather. It is a good idea to scope out the possibilities in advance and keep an eye on a likely source. When the nut is ready for harvest, the outer hull will split open and the brown-shelled pecan will fall to the ground. If you find nuts still in their hull, don't bother with them. They are not ripe or good. Look for signs of insect or squirrel damage and avoid those nuts as well. Pick up the nuts and let them dry naturally for a little while. A completely dry shell will be easier to crack, and the nuts will be ready to use. Nuts will keep in the shell for several months. Keep them in a cool, dry place. Every pecan lover has a

Pecans on the ground in public places are free for the taking.

favorite nut cracker. It can be as simple as a hammer or as fancy as an electric smacking device. The trick is to find a way to get the shell off without smashing the nut. Pecan shells are not nearly as hard as walnut or hickory shells, so be gentle. Lots of folks squeeze two nuts together in their hands to crack and eat them on the spot. Shelled pecans keep well in the freezer. Put them in freezer containers as soon as you shell them; then use what you need and leave the rest frozen.

Toasted pecans are a great addition to almost any dish. They are particularly good sprinkled on salads. A favorite fall treat is spinach salad with "Ruby Red" grapefruit sections sprinkled with toasted pecans and dressed with a vinaigrette dressing. Of course, the great pecan classic is pie. There are many variations on the theme. This is my mother's recipe. I have used molasses and honey and brown sugar, and each gives a slightly different flavor. The essentials are pecans and sweetness, and nothing is better.

MOTHER'S PECAN PIE

3 eggs
1 cup sugar
¾ cup white Karo syrup
2 tablespoons flour
¼ cup butter
1 cup pecans, chopped or whole
1 teaspoon vanilla

Preheat oven to 400°F. Beat eggs until light. Add other ingredients and pour into unbaked pie shell (see following recipe). Bake 15 minutes. Reduce heat to 350°F and cook about 45 minutes longer until a knife inserted into the center comes out clean.

MOTHER'S HOT-WATER PIE CRUST

½ cup boiling water
½ cup shortening
1½ cups flour
½ teaspoon salt
½ teaspoon baking powder

Pour water over shortening and beat until creamy. Sift flour with salt and baking powder. Mix together quickly with a fork and roll out on a floured board. Place in pie plate and fill.

Food trends come and go as do all trends, and right now foraging is once again cool. Euell Gibbons sold thousands of copies of his book *Stalking the Wild Asparagus* in the 1960s and sparked an interest in wild foods that has waxed and waned in the years since. Whether because of the interest in local foods or the need to save money, foraging is a popular trend in both cities and rural areas. Upscale restaurants and gourmet publications are including recipes and dishes with ingredients found growing in cracks in the sidewalk and along creeks. Purslane, a succulent formerly known as a weed, is a popular salad green and full of nutrition. Chickweed, miner's lettuce, plantain, and ramps are all popular wild foods that can be foraged and enjoyed.

The problem with foraging is that people can get overly enthusiastic and strip the plant to extinction. In many places wild coneflowers (*Echinacea* SPP.) have been so overpicked that the plants have been destroyed. Be sure to leave healthy plants behind to continue to grow and flourish. Tread lightly when you venture into the countryside. Before you set out to forage for wild food, you need to do some homework.

Learn what grows in your area and know how to identify it—for sure! Don't take any chances. Wild mushrooms, for example, are tasty treats, but there are many poisonous mushrooms that look very much like the edible kind. If you aren't sure, don't take a chance. When we first moved from the city to the country, I found garlic growing along the road. It was obviously garlic, smelled and looked like it, but I asked a new neighbor to make sure. "Yeah," he said, "that's that old ditch garlic . . . unless of course it is the death lily." Ha ha ha, rural humor. Still, I looked close to make sure it was garlic. It was, and its offspring are growing in my garden today, 20 years later.

Once you know what you have, think about where it is growing. If it is growing beside a stream, make sure the water isn't polluted. If it is grow-ing beside the road, make sure the county hasn't been spraying poisons on the verge. Of course, you won't forage on private land, and when you find something good, be sure to wash it several times before eating it.

Ditch garlic has become a domesticated, reliable, and tasty essential in the kitchen.

Finally, when you have found an edible, be sure you know how to prepare it. Some greens like pokeweed need to be cooked in several changes
of water or they will cause stomach upsets. Here is a list of wild greens
and herbs that grow in the United States (find out which ones grow near
you): chickweed, chicory, curly dock, dandelion, fiddlehead, lamb's quar-
ters, miner's lettuce, nettle, peppercress, pigweed, plantain, pokeweed,
purslane, sorrel, watercress, wild asparagus, wild horsemint (bee balm),
and wild mustard.

In some areas of the country you can find wild fruits that are wonder-
fully delicious. Every year I gather wild mustang grapes for jelly, and my
husband has been known to make passable wine from the juice. Other
wild fruits include strawberries, raspberries, blackberries (dewberries),
blueberries, mulberries, juneberries, serviceberries, chokeberries, elder-
berries, wild cherries, wild plums, gooseberries, buffalo currants, persimmons, rose hips, prickly pear fruit, and pawpaws. Find out which ones
grow in your area and when they ripen. Wild grapes are ripe in our area
in early July, but other berries are much earlier.

Blueberry bush and berries.

Many places have local treasures that grow only in limited areas. Snoop, ask, and discover the tasty treats that may be lurking nearby. Fish fall into this category, although we are focusing on edible plants. Fish are good and good for you and abundant in lakes, rivers, and oceans around the country. All it takes is a license and a line to reel in dinner.

Forest Gardening

Forest gardening is a low-maintenance, sustainable way to grow food. It is also one of the oldest known ways that people have grown food for themselves. Food forests combine trees, vines, perennial, and annual food plants such as herbs, fruit, and some vegetables in a woodland setting. They are common in tropical regions where unwanted plants are removed from the native environment and desirable plants encouraged. The term "forest gardening" was coined in England by Robert Hart, who was interested in providing a healthy and therapeutic environment for himself and others. He described a system based on his observation of the layers in a native forest. He suggested turning an orchard into a seven-layer garden to provide much food with less effort and smaller space than a large farm. On top was the "canopy layer," which consisted of mature fruit or nut trees. Next comes the "low-tree layer" made up of fruit and nuts growing on dwarfing rootstocks that keep them small. The third layer, "shrubs," consists of fruit bushes such as berries. The fourth, "herbaceous layer," is made up of perennial vegetables and herbs—asparagus, artichoke, adapted herbs. The fifth layer is the "rhizosphere" or underground dimension of plants that are grown for their roots and tubers—potatoes, sweet potatoes, onions, garlic, and such. The sixth layer consists of "ground cover" plants that spread horizontally across the soil, either annuals or perennials. The last is the "vertical layer" made up of vines and climbers, again either perennial or annual. For this system to work, the plants must be selected so they can tolerate some shade and are adapted to the climate where they are growing.

Books and articles have been written about forest gardening. Permaculture, a style of gardening relying on layers of perennial crops that support and maintain each other, is a related system. Throughout the world people are experimenting with forest gardens. Seattle, Washington, boasts the largest US food forest, the 7-acre Beacon Food Forest that uses public land to produce food for citizens. Other cities and towns have put and are putting in master-planned food forests on public land. In Austin, Texas, a new master-planned food forest is being created in a public park. Two acres of city parkland are being transformed into a forest garden where people can enjoy the land, encourage growth of trees and other plants, and share the harvest. It will include fruit and nut trees, a rainwater harvesting system, permaculture beds, and wetlands. Food forests not only provide food, but they save water, fight air pollution by growing air-cleaning trees in urban areas, and produce a refuge for wildlife.

7 If You Want to do More, Go to Bed(s)

If, having grown some lettuce in a pot and some strawberries in a galvanized tub, you decide this gardening thing is pretty good fun and tasty too, there are lots of ways to add more growing space to your yard.

Raised Beds

While many gardeners clear an area and plant directly in the ground, in other cases raised beds are easier and more productive. If you have poor soil, rocky soil, or no soil, then raised beds are the answer. Raised beds let you put your garden where you want it and where it will receive maxi-

Raised beds are easy to construct and maintain.

mum light. They also allow you to build nutritious, rich soil by buying or amending soil so that it has what is necessary to grow good food. You can plant veggies or fruit in raised beds. Traditional raised beds can be simply piled above ground level with gradually slanting sides, or they can be bordered to hold in the soil. Borders can be almost any material: wood in the form of logs, lumber, or landscape timbers; metal; stone; concrete blocks; bricks; or other material. You want the siding to be sturdy so it will last several years, and you want it to be nontoxic. Some wood has been treated to protect it from insects and/or weathering, and the chemicals will leach into the soil and hence into your food. Use aged wood or wood you know has not been treated or logs cut from a fallen tree.

Sheet Composting

If you want to plant in a new area, fall is the best time to prepare the soil—but you don't have to get out the shovel. Instead, select your spot and sheet compost the area. Here's how: Outline the spot where you want your new planting area. You can trench around the area if you wish, but it is not necessary. You can also build walls of wood, concrete blocks, or other material to hold the soil you are building in place. Water the ground well where you want your new bed.

Using cardboard sheets (preferably unprinted) or black-and-white newspaper sheets, completely cover the area. Large boxes in which appliances are shipped are excellent, because it takes only a few to cover a large area. Make sure you overlap the sheets so that all soil, weeds, and grass are covered. If you are using newspaper, use several layers. Thoroughly wet the cardboard or paper.

Next, add about 4 inches of manure on top of the cardboard or paper. Thoroughly soak the manure once it is in place. The manure can come from cattle, horses, chickens, or sheep, and it need not be composted first. Check with stables, farms, or other local sources for fresh manure. Before you load up the manure, ask about whether the animals have been given antibiotics or drugs. Antibiotics in the manure will kill your soil, serving the opposite purpose that the manure is designed to serve.

Finally, add a layer of mulch about 12 inches deep. Straw or leaves are good choices. Leaves are usually readily available in the fall, and they are lightweight and easy to handle. In addition, they bring with them the nutrients from deep in the ground in which the trees were grown. Thoroughly wet the mulch and then let nature take its course.

The cardboard or paper layer acts as a barrier to the grass or weeds underneath and smothers the plants. The manure adds richness to the area and helps break down the cardboard and the mulch. It also encourages the growth of microorganisms in the soil that will feed your plants. By the time spring arrives, the cardboard will be disintegrated enough so that you can pull aside some of the mulch, dig into the rich new soil, and place your new plants. You will have a nice new bed without the backbreaking work of spading up the area. Add new mulch as the old breaks down, and you have created a wonderful new planting area with very little work.

Variations on a Theme

If you don't want a standard raised bed garden, there are a lot of other choices. Keyhole gardens are popular with people who don't want to or can't bend over. The idea behind these gardens is that you build a mostly circular raised bed with a notch in the side so that you can just walk in and tend your crops. You can buy ready-made or kits for keyhole gardens made of metal and other materials, or you can build your own with rocks or wood. Look online to see different styles of keyhole gardens and choose one that works for you. Size will depend on how much room you

Keyhole garden at the Helping Center garden in Marble Falls, Texas.

Malcolm Beck, founder of Garden-Ville, makes raised beds from tractor tires.

want and how long your arms are. You want to be able to reach all of the bed either from the sides or from the keyhole. Because you fill this garden with rich soil, you can grow a lot of produce in a small amount of space. It is a good idea to build a compost pile in the center of the garden so that the bed is constantly feeding itself and you always have a spot to put garden waste. Simply put a wire circular container in the middle of the bed on the ground and extend it above the level of the raised bed. Water through this center, and the moisture will distribute evenly and take with it nutrients coming from the rotting compost. The center compost well will also provide a bit of extra warmth during cold weather and can be a support for row cover to protect crops growing in cool seasons.

The sides of the keyhole garden must be sealed well enough to hold in soil and moisture. If you use bricks or stones for the outside walls, be sure they fit together tightly so that soil will not wash away during rain or watering. You can start by lining the walls with cardboard to hold in the soil while the whole bed settles into its final shape. You can also use bamboo or other sticks woven into a fence for your siding or experiment with materials readily available in your area.

Hugelkultur, a German word, describes a system of building raised beds filled with rotting wood. You can build these beds in a variety of ways, including the keyhole style. If you do that, simply fill the bottom half or more of your bed with old logs, sticks, and various-sized pieces of wood. The wood should be old, and the more rotten the better. Adding this organic material to the soil you put on top will provide for great drainage, air pockets for roots to infiltrate, water conservation, and a source of continued nutrition as the wood breaks down. If your wood is relatively new, you might want to add a layer of green material on top—kitchen waste, trimmings from plants, leaves—to ensure that there is enough nitrogen in the pile to feed your plants and to speed up the composting of the logs.

Hugelkultur gardens are a great way to use up rotting wood, twigs, branches, and other tree parts that might otherwise go to the dump. The easiest way to build this kind of garden is to simply pile the wood, largest pieces on the bottom, on top of your existing yard. Add a layer of nitrogen-rich material on top of the logs. Top and fill in with good soil and begin planting. It can be built with or without a border. Remember that wood is carbon and can use up nutrients as it decays, so add some nitrogen in the form of manure, green garden waste, and organic fertilizer until the wood becomes well rotted. Your bed can be a rounded mound or a tidy rectangle. Whichever way you go, you'll find that this kind of garden saves on water, gets better with time, and is really easy to build. As always, check with other local gardeners to see how their experiences and experiments can help you avoid their mistakes.

The cylinder gardening program was begun in 1986 under the leadership of the Men's Garden Club of Houston, the Harris County Master Gardener Association, and the Texas A&M AgriLife Extension Service's Horticulture Program in Harris County, Texas. Cylinder gardening uses bottomless cylinders (half of a 4- or 5-gallon food-grade bucket) as small, individual gardens for growing vegetables. This works especially well in areas with poor soil that normally need extensive amendments and labor to support an actively producing garden. The program is great for school-age children and can be used in classrooms, after-school programs, and home schools or with other groups and clubs as well as home gardens. Cylinder gardening requires little land and little pregardening preparation or experience. Once the cylinders are filled and planted, the only labor is minor maintenance, watering, and harvesting. Plants mature from seed in 30 to 90 days. Installation and removal of the garden are quick and clean. When using this method, you simply cut the bottom out of the bucket or cut it in half. Poke the open end into the ground and fill it with good soil. Plant your seeds. By the time the weeds have figured out how to get into the bucket, it is time to harvest. Simply remove the buckets and reuse another time and perhaps another place.

Malcolm Beck, founder of Garden-Ville, grows raised bed gardens in tractor tires. All that is necessary is to put down some sort of weed block—cardboard or landscape cloth—and roll the tire into place. You can use smaller tires. Fill the tires with good soil, and you are ready to go. Malcolm lines them up and fills them with flowers and vegetables.

Another variation on the container/raised bed theme is the straw bale garden, in which straw bales are the growing medium. The straw will decompose as the plants grow, providing nutrients. To prepare your straw bed garden, put landscape fabric down to keep weeds from growing into the bales. Arrange as many bales as you want in rows on the fabric with the string sides facing out and the unstrung side facing up. Water and fertilize the bales for about 2 weeks before you want to plant. For the first 6 days put 3 cups of organic fertilizer on each bale every other day and water well. Use water only on the other days. On days 7–9 add 1½ cups of fertilizer each day and water well. On day 10 put 3 cups of bone or fish meal mixed with ½ cup wood ash and again water thoroughly. You should begin to see signs of composting soon. Mushrooms are a good sign.

It is a good idea to build a trellis above the bales to let your plants grow up rather than sprawl on the ground. Use posts of any type at the end of each row and run wire between them at intervals of 10 inches above the top of the bales. Pull the top of the bales apart enough so you can insert young seedlings into the straw with a little bit of potting soil to cover the roots. You can plant flowers or herbs in the sides of the bales. Drape a soaker hose over the top of the bales and water when they become dry. All you have to do then is wait until harvest time. The biggest caveat here is that you really need *straw* bales, not *hay* bales. Hay contains seeds that are good for horses and cows when they eat it but not good for your vegetable garden. Straw is easier to find in some areas than others. Be sure you know what you are getting when you buy bales. Once the harvest is complete, push your bales together and voilà—a compost pile!

Spiral gardens are based on concepts that came from the permaculture gardening movement. In these gardens crops support each other by sharing space, nutrients, and water. The beds can be built high or low, large or small. The center of the bed is always higher than the outside, and the spiral can go around as many times as you want or space allows. Build your bed from the ground up, raising the elevation as you go around the circle. A layer of gravel on the ground will help with drainage if you have naturally heavy or damp soil. As the spiral gets higher, the gravel will also add stability to the bed. Fill in the spiral as you build it with good, rich soil. When it is finished, water it well and allow the soil to settle. Once that has happened, you can begin to plant. Keep in mind that plants at the top will drain more quickly than ones at the bottom. Consider how tall the plants will grow as they mature and take into account any shade they will share with neighboring plants. Also leave room for them to grow outward as well as upward. Some people plant herb spirals, using various kinds of herbs to fill the spaces.

Wicking gardens are self-contained beds with built-in reservoirs that supply water from the bottom up. Wicking beds are water efficient since no evaporation occurs at the surface level. They water themselves when they need watering, and there is no problem with poor drainage since they capture and use rain only when it is needed. The water is wicked upward through some sort of material that will gather moisture and dispense it when it is needed. Wicking beds are more expensive to build than other types of beds because they require more material. You can find directions for building the beds online, or you can find a local source for either bed-building instructions or ready-made beds. They can be large, constructed, permanent installations or the size of a plastic storage container that you make yourself or any size in between.

Garden Anywhere Boxes are wicking gardens for sale and ready to be hooked up to your rainwater collection system or your outdoor faucet so that they water themselves. You can have as many or as few of these bins as you want and save yourself the trouble of weeding and watering while enjoying the delights of harvesting.

Which brings us to the many kinds of purchased gardens that are available these days. You can buy big containers to fill with dirt for instant gardens. They can be made of synthetic material so they are light to move. Some are fabric and can be folded up in a small bag for stor-

Garden Anywhere Boxes can be purchased and filled with only minimum labor.

age. Others are rigid and semi-permanent. You can also decide that some variation on the hydroponics theme is right for you.

Hydroponics and Aquaponics

Hydroponics, aquaponics, and "ponics" in between are systems in which the plants grow in enriched water. Hydroponics systems have been around for a long time and have generally been used by commercial producers, but today home hydroponics systems are flourishing. You can set up your system on a porch, patio, or balcony or even indoors if you invest in lights as well as the system. Although some people can probably create their own hydroponics system, most will purchase them. The least expensive range just over one hundred dollars for systems that will grow a few plants. As the growing space increases, so does the cost. Tower systems allow for much more space and are interesting looking when they are covered with plants, but they look like a big chunk of plastic when they are not. In addition to the cost of the original unit, you will have to continue to purchase chemicals to feed your plants.

Tabletop aquaponics system. Photo courtesy of Friendly Aquaponics.

Aquaponics systems include fish in the mix. Fish swim in the water, adding their waste, which is then used by the plants as fertilizer. It is a continuous loop—water to plants to fish to plants to fish and on and on. Friendly Aquaponics, based in Hawaii, offers advice, instruction, and help in setting up systems ranging from a table-top variety shown in the picture to a commercial-sized operation for professional growers. Other systems are available in different areas. Check to see if there are options in your locale.

Malcolm Beck has been using an aquaponics system for years. He has tanks of tilapia in his greenhouse with hanging pots over the tanks. Pumps circulate and aerate the water and move it up into the pots, where the nutrients are removed as fertilizer for the plants and then cleaned water drips back into the tanks. He can eat the produce grown in the pots and the fish too. It is an elegant system that is a lot simpler than many complicated systems offered commercially.

The Amazing Above Ground Garden was developed by an entre-preneur and gardener in Texas. In this system plants grow in soil and reclaimed water. Lightweight and easy to put together, the kit is intensive gardening at eye level. The kits come in three sizes, are easy to put together, and include everything you need, even a hammer. See what bright ideas are being created in your area and experiment with your own inventions.

Browsing through the choices in a nice big local nursery is fun and a little daunting. You may also find some new options at farmers' markets and spring or fall plant festivals. There are so many! It is fun to imagine yourself with all kinds of delicious produce at the tip of your fingers. You can pick one and give it a try. On the other hand, you can always stick to a simple system of dirt in ground, tomato in pot, cash at the farmers' market.

The Amazing Above Ground Garden offers a compact space for several kinds of food.

Hydroponic tower gardens are an investment that once set up are nearly labor-free.

8   Taking the Show on the Road

GARDENING AWAY FROM HOME

We've talked about several ways you can grow food without having a garden in the ground, but some folks want a garden in the ground. They just don't have space or sun for one. If you would like your own little garden bed with good soil and bright sunshine but live where those things are unavailable, don't despair. Opportunities abound where you can do your gardening in somebody else's yard. Just inquire locally!

Community Gardens

The first community garden in the United States was established in 1893 in Detroit. A plot of empty, unused land was set aside for unemployed people to plant and grow food. Through the years interest in using land in cities for gardening has grown. In many places, people have taken the initiative and cleaned up trashy lots and abandoned plots and begun planting there. Community gardens are particularly important in large cities where people are less likely to have large yards for gardening.

Even in small towns, they serve a purpose. If you don't have room at home to garden, look for a community garden nearby. Community gardens generally provide space, water, and help getting started. Some have compost piles that are available to all gardeners. Plot size varies from very small to pretty large. Some community gardens have a big garden where food is grown for the local food bank. Many have in-ground beds that you can design to suit yourself. Others have a series of raised beds, and everyone who participates uses one of them. Some beds are designed to be accessible to people in wheelchairs.

Each community garden has its own rules as well as its own layout. Some request that you give a portion of your harvest to the food bank. Others charge a minimal fee for renting space. Most gardens are begun

Community gardens come
in all shapes and sizes.

by volunteers who want space to garden themselves, and the project is coordinated with the landowner, in many cases the city. Generally gardens require the use of organic methods and have a few other rules: the garden must be kept clean, the beds must be planted and maintained, and food must be the main crop although flowers are welcome to encourage pollinators. Beds can be adopted by individuals, families, or groups like Boy or Girl Scout troops. There is usually a blend of experienced and beginning gardeners and young and old people.

Although begun with a goal of helping people feed themselves, community gardens have often grown into much more. There is at least as much emphasis on "community" as there is on "garden." They provide a place for neighbors to meet each other and interact. They encourage exercise and outdoor activity while beautifying the neighborhood. And of course, they provide nutritious food for people who might otherwise not have access to it. Lydia Roman of East Harlem summarizes well the special effort of community gardening: "If you had seen that trash-filled lot, you'd have said it would take a miracle to make a garden. In time and with much hard work we accomplished the impossible. Now we have something beautiful to look at . . . flowers, fruits, and vegetables for the community. When people walk by, they compliment the garden. One surprised person said, 'It's magic.' So we called the garden the Magic Garden, but in reality, the magic is within us."

The ways that communities can garden together is limited only by the imagination. For example, some neighborhood gardens have developed naturally by neighbors sharing their land and talents. In one neighborhood, Pat and Leslie have a big yard and love fresh food, but their health and age limit the work they can do in the garden, so their neighbors who are younger but live in a much smaller place trade their time and energy to build a garden in Pat and Leslie's yard. They all share the produce. The idea can spread throughout the neighborhood with people contributing space or compost or digging or harvesting or canning or whatever they decide. The result is lots of good food and a healthy neighborhood community.

Gardens Here, There, and Everywhere

Gardens can spring up just about anywhere. Many schools have gardens that teach the children about food and gardening and give them a chance to dig in the dirt. All of these gardens welcome volunteers, who share in the fun and the rewards.

The Escoffier School of Culinary Arts in Austin has a 6,000-square-foot garden that was once a parking lot. It includes raised beds, wicking beds, beds in the ground, and hydroponic beds. The students participate in the growing and then in the cooking of the produce, learning how to prepare food as well as where it comes from.

In Boulder, Colorado, the Children's Peace Garden serves children ages three to ten. It is designed to teach children about nature, the source of food, and gardening and give them a chance to have some good fun in the dirt. The garden offers spring and fall field trips and classroom visits to schools throughout the city, a summer camp, and an after-school garden club.

Mesa, Arizona, has a nonprofit garden in the heart of downtown. Mesa Urban Garden (MUG) is proof that the desert can bloom. The garden offers more than one hundred beds, including accessible beds for people with disabilities, that are leased to individuals, groups, or sponsors. In addition to individual beds, there is a communal area that is tended by volunteers, and the food is available to food banks and folks in need. This garden provides a raised bed garden, good soil, drip irrigation system, watering timer, and help. The cost depends on the size of the bed.

Some churches have also established gardens. Grace Church in Old Saybrook, Connecticut, gardens a quarter acre of land and donates the produce to a local soup kitchen and food bank. The Lutheran Church of Our Redeemer in Sacramento, California, turned an empty church lot into Redeemer's Field, a source of healthful and affordable food that encourages parishioners and others to enjoy the fun of growing their own. The city's Parks and Recreation Department helped the church establish this community garden and others around the town.

Look around your world and see what the opportunities may be. The "community" in community gardens can be any group that wants to work together to accomplish a goal of fresh food. It can be defined by the location—city, neighborhood, or block—or it can be a group of individuals linked by a common cause or interest—ballet dancers, yoga class, bridge club, or reading group. Community gardens come in all shapes and sizes, but in every case they serve the community by creating beautiful spaces and good food.

Ask local gardening groups what they know. The Master Gardeners in Marble Falls, Texas, have established a beautiful food garden next to the local food bank, the Helping Center. They grow all kinds of vegetables and some fruit. The produce goes to the food bank, and the gardeners have a good time producing it. Health can come not only from the food but also from the process of growing it.

9   Just Get It!

A big part of the reward of growing your own food comes from the taste, health, and freshness of the resulting produce. Even if you do grow in flower beds, pots, and the kitchen, you may still not have all the fresh food you want. That's when a little ingenuity and adventure enter the process. Seek out places to find fresh, healthy, and local food. Go for a nice Saturday drive in the country and come home with a basketful of goodies. There are many options for finding good food that don't involve any digging, planting, or watering. In addition to filling your pantry wish list, these options also support the people who are making their living as farmers. Local farmers need us all to support their efforts. It is another way of being involved in agriculture.

Pick Your Own

Throughout the country there are farmers who invite you to come onto their farm and select the fresh produce that looks just right for you. Berries, fruit, vegetables, and even eggs can be part of the "pick your own" experience. Look online (start with pickyourown.org) to find a farm near you that encourages picking. It is a fun experience, and you end up with the freshest food possible.

Think about what is seasonal when you think about picking your own. For example, lots of places have pumpkin patches around harvest time where you can not only find pumpkins but also corn mazes, hayrides, and other fun stuff. If it is apple season and apples grow in your neck of the woods, search out growers that let you come pick in their orchards. You might even find a pick-your-own farm by visiting a local farmers' market. Farmers have to make a living by diversifying, so letting you come pick is a possibility. It can't hurt to ask.

Picking blueberries is fun for all.

There are a few rules to remember about picking your own. Most important is that you must respect the farmer and the farm. Be careful of the plants, watch where you walk, and ask before you start if there are rules to be followed. Some farms are very casual, and others are more structured. It is up to the farmer to decide what works and up to you to follow those rules.

As you pick, be careful with the plants. Try hard not to break stems, limbs, or vines. Don't step on plants or fruit. If you brought kids (and it is a great thing for kids to do), help them learn to be respectful of the farm and the plants. Try not to pick unripened fruit and then toss it on the ground. Choose the produce you want and leave the rest in good condition for the next picker.

It is a good idea to wear long pants, long-sleeved shirts, and sensible shoes when you go harvesting. Some plants, like blackberries, grow on thorny bushes that will scratch your arms if they aren't covered. Other crops, like okra, really need to be picked early in the morning because they get more irritating to the skin as the day heats up. In patches where the bushes are no threat, there can be ants, other biting insects, and even snakes on the ground. It is best to be aware of your surroundings and protect your body with clothing. Some farms are very tidy, and there is very little cover on the ground. Others are weedy with places for critters to hide. Just keep your eyes open. There is very little hazard of biting snakes or other dangerous animals. They will be scared away by the talking and walking people.

While most farmers provide containers to put your pickings in, it is a good idea to take a cooler with you to transport your goodies home. Every fruit and veggie will keep better if it is cool. The blueberry farm in the photographs provides pickers with a harness and bucket to allow both hands to be free for picking. The bucket holds a gallon, and you can get as many or as few as you want. This farm charges by the pint. Others may charge by the pound. When you are done and your produce has been measured and paid for, you need a container to put it in. The bucket stays behind at the farm. A bag will do, or a bag that goes into the cooler is even better.

Don't expect big bargains at pick-your-own farms. After all, picking is an adventure and an outing. There is entertainment value here as well as produce. The farmer has to do extra work to make his or her field safe for strangers to venture into. He also has to allow for produce consumed on the premises—you cannot pick blueberries or strawberries without popping a few into your mouth. And she has to advertise, buy buckets, and put up signs. So consider picking your own an adventure and pay the price. It won't be cheap, but it won't be exorbitant either. It will be much less expensive than going to the movies and a lot better for you!

If you are looking for fruit that is delicious, easy to prepare, and extremely nutritious, how about blueberries? They don't need peeling, pitting, coring, or slicing. Pop them in your mouth raw or use them in recipes. Stick them in the freezer or make jam. Blueberries are packed with antioxidants and other things to make you healthy, so there is no excuse not to enjoy blueberries in season. Blueberries are popular with lots of folks, but they are not often grown in home gardens. That is where pick-your-own farms come in. Be sure to contact the farm by e-mail, website, or phone before you go to make sure it is open and

Ella, Braxton, Trenton, and Bailey have been strawberry picking at Star Farmers Market in Rockdale, Texas, since they started walking.

berries are ready. Plants operate on their own schedule, not the plans of people. Berries may be ripe in April one year and May the next. To save yourself time and frustration, make sure you find out in advance.

At Bill McCranie's Chickamaw Farm in Bastrop County where we picked blueberries, there were people of all ages, all shapes and sizes, and all lifestyles. It was a genial and fun group who talked about why they were there, how they found out about it (the Internet), and what their previous experiences were as blueberry pickers. One young woman said she worked for her uncle on his blueberry farm in Michigan when she was in high school and ate her weight in berries every summer. A little girl inspected each berry seriously and carefully before dropping it into her bucket. Two muscled and tattooed men from Chicago had also picked with their grandmother when they were young. Three generations of one family were there picking together and instructing each other on how to do it best. Obviously a lot of the pickers were regulars and knew each other. They did as much visiting as they did picking. It was a wonderful way to spend a June morning and support a local farmer, plus we had delicious blueberries to eat fresh and freeze so that the rewards lasted for a nice long time.

Blueberries grow all over the country. K&D U-Pick Blueberries, located near Woodstock, Alabama, uses no pesticides on their farm. They begin allowing picking in mid- to late June and continue until the berries are done. Alabama even has a blueberry festival on the third Saturday in June in Brewton. The festival features arts and crafts, entertainment for kids and adults, an antique car and motorcycle show, and the stars of the day: fresh blueberries and blueberry bushes.

One pick-your-own option that is well worth your support if you are in the area is the Veterans Farm in Jacksonville, Florida. Home of the "red, white, and blueberry", this project was designed to provide a healing atmosphere for returning veterans while teaching them good, marketable agricultural skills. The farm has multiple goals: to help reintegrate veterans into society, prepare veterans with the tools for a successful agriculture career, and provide good healthy food. They partner with the University of Florida extension educators to provide a 3-month intensive training course to prepare vets to start their own farm or work for another farmer. Using sustainable methods, the farm produces pick-your-own blueberries, already-picked blueberries, frozen blueberries, and blueberry bushes plus herbs and peppers. The founders of this farm hope to expand the idea into other areas to give veterans who may be physically or emotionally challenged the opportunity to enjoy the healing benefits of working with nature while learning new skills. You can learn more by visiting www.veteransfarm.org or visiting the farm in Jacksonville.

The Bostwick Blueberry Festival in Florida gives you an opportunity to see how other folks use fresh blueberries. They offer a blueberry pancake breakfast, blueberry ice cream, and homemade blueberry pies, along with other fun. After you enjoy pancakes, pie, and ice cream, you can pick some fresh berries to take home at Alachua County Organic Farms in Micanopy, Florida, or Berry Bay Farm, which offers organic berries near Earleton, Florida. BlueBela Farm has garnered rave reviews on the Internet. The farm uses no pesticides and offers a chance for you to pick berries, buy berries they have picked, or have a party on the grounds. It is located near Gainesville, Florida, in High Springs.

You can find all sorts of delicious produce at pick-your-own farms: blackberries, strawberries, raspberries, squash, lettuce, onions, pumpkins, tomatoes, and anything and everything that can be grown on a farm. Not every farm will grow every crop, but almost anything is available as pick your own if you look. As a matter of fact, once you start browsing the listing, you'll want to plan your vacations by traveling from one picking spot to the next. In addition to picking, many farms offer other good things: local honey, eggs, meat, cheese, spots for picnics and parties, perhaps some farm animals with whom to discuss the issues of the day. A visit to a farm is a great way to spend the day with or without kids, and having something delicious to take home is an added bonus.

Farmers' Markets

Almost every town has a farmers' market. It can be a big beautiful affair or a couple of farmers with their pickup trucks in a parking lot. Whatever form it takes, it is a great opportunity to find fresh, local, seasonal, and often sustainably grown food. Shopping at farmers' markets is also a way to support farmers in your area, since they get full value for their food. Usually a market sets up once or twice each week, and the number of farmers will vary depending on their schedule and how much they have to sell that day. The products will vary as well, depending on what is in season.

In the past few years farmers' markets have expanded to include not only fresh produce but other products grown or created locally. You can find fresh or frozen meat at most markets. Generally, the meat is grown without hormones or other chemicals and comes from a farm nearby. Pork, beef, and chicken plus some more exotic meats such as venison and a variety of sausages are often available. In some cases, the meat is offered ready to eat: pulled pork tacos, beef sandwiches, or barbecued chicken. Other homemade items include breads, cakes, pies and cookies, jams and jellies, gelato, olive and pecan oils, pickles, local cheeses, flavored vinegars, and more. Ethnic foods of Mexican, Indian, and African origin are also sometimes ready to take home for dinner or eat on the spot.

Don't limit yourself to the closest market. Check out as many markets as are readily accessible. Each one is different, with different foods and different ambience. Some have live music—sometimes it is awful music; sometimes it is great. In either case, it is a conversation starter. Some are held outdoors in a parking lot; others are inside a barn or under a spread of old trees. Be sure to take cash with you. Most markets take food stamps as well as vouchers from WIC. Remember to take some reusable bags to carry all your great loot. If the farmer isn't covered up with customers, take a minute to chat. Farmers are happy to tell you about what they grow, where they grow it, and why. And don't forget to tell them that you appreciate their labors. Everyone needs that from time to time.

Farm Stands

Some farmers whose farms are easily accessible simply put up a farm stand and sell from there. Some haul their goods to a nearby road and put up a stand. There are also people who go buy food from the local wholesaler and put up a stand somewhere. If the stand isn't on the farm, ask where the produce comes from and who grows it. You might be surprised. Such items as bananas and coconuts are a sure sign that the produce isn't grown locally.

Farmers' markets.

Boggy Creek Farms farmstand. Photo courtesy of Carole Ann Sayles.

In many areas, urban farms sell directly to consumers. Austin has a lively urban farm community that includes both old and new farms. Boggy Creek Farm, just a few miles from the bustle of downtown, has been selling fresh, organically grown vegetables since 1992. Larry Butler and Carol Ann Sayle took a very old and neglected farm and turned it into a showplace where they welcome visitors and customers several days each week. Boggy Creek is a certified organic farm. They sell their fresh food to neighbors, people from across Central Texas, and many local chefs. They have since been joined by other city farmers who offer fresh food, a bed-and-breakfast, eggs, artisan baked goods, and more. The fun of buying directly from the farms is that you not only get to meet the farmers but you get to see where the food is grown, have a word with the chickens, and select the special treats each farmer has to offer.

Potomac Vegetable Farms (PVF) began in the 1960s as a small family farm near Washington, D.C. Over the years the farm has grown in size and production. It produces its crops using what it calls "Ecoganic," a term coined to reflect organic methods and sustainability that is not regulated by federally mandated programs. The farm was certified organic in 1990 by the state of Virginia, but when federal certification began in 2004, they decided to continue their old practices but avoid the new paperwork and complications. The goal of certification was to let consumers know how food is grown and processed. The farm does that itself. Today PVF has two farm stands on major roadways, sells at several farmers' markets, and offers the opportunity for consumers to join their CSA (see the next section). PVF stands sell their own produce plus pies, soup, jams, jellies, and honey. They also carry other local products, including herbs, flowers, mushrooms, meat, and fruit.

Community Supported Agriculture (CSA)

In addition to setting up stands and going to farmers' markets, some farmers offer the option of a CSA (Community Supported Agriculture). CSAs were dreamed up to give farmers a little bit of security in their very insecure profession. People join the group and agree to pay a certain amount each week for their produce. The farmer then has a good idea of income and can plan accordingly. Some farmers deliver. Others let you pick up your box. Every subscriber gets the same items, although sometimes you can add non-produce items such as eggs or bread.

While many farmers who offer CSAs also sell at farmers' markets or farm stands, the CSA is their bread and butter and hedge against poor sales in other locations. These farmers offer a wide variety of foods, sometimes rare varieties that you are not apt to find anywhere else. Organic and heirloom vegetables are common in these boxes.

CSAs are not confined to produce. Some farmers include the option for shareholders to buy shares of eggs, homemade bread, meat, cheese, fruit, flowers, or other farm products along with their veggies. Sometimes several farmers will offer their products together, to offer the widest variety to their members. For example, a produce farmer might create a partnership with a neighbor to deliver chickens to the CSA drop-off point so that the CSA members can purchase farm-fresh chickens when they come to get their baskets. Other farmers are creating stand-alone CSAs for meat, flowers, eggs, and preserved farm products.

In some parts of the country, nonfarming third parties are setting up CSA-like businesses, where they act as middlemen and sell boxes of local (and sometimes not local) food for their members. Some of these co-ops offer local food; some do not. Some also give you an organic or nonorganic option. Always ask before joining a group about where the food comes from and how it is grown.

Although having choices is sometimes fun, it is also sometimes wearying. With most CSAs, you get what you get (and don't throw a fit!). It offers you the opportunity to try new things and expand your culinary repertoire. Usually the CSA will offer recipes and tips on preparing the food that comes in the box. Many have newsletters that go to subscribers. Subscribers sometimes share their recipes and experiences with each other through a newsletter or website.

As with all farming efforts, variations are legion. Some CSAs want you to come help pull weeds and harvest. Other definitely do not. Some offer food year-round; others are seasonal. Some offer standard boxes, and some put out the week's harvest and let members fill their own boxes. Subscribers often become a community unto themselves, feeling involved in the well-being of the farm and the farmers. Kids often say they like the food from "their farm" better than any other food.

There is an important concept woven into the CSA model that takes the arrangement beyond the usual commercial transaction. That is the notion of shared risk: in most CSAs, members pay up front for the whole season, and the farmers do their best to provide an abundant box of produce each week. If harvests are slim, members are not typically reimbursed. The result is a feeling of "we're in this together." On some farms the idea of shared risk is stronger than others, and CSA members may be asked to sign a policy form indicating that they agree to accept without complaint whatever the farm can produce.

Many times, the idea of shared risk is part of what creates a sense of community among members, and between members and the farmers. If a hailstorm takes out all the peppers, everyone is disappointed together, and together cheer on the winter squash and broccoli. Most CSA farmers feel a great sense of responsibility to their members, and when certain crops are scarce, they make sure the CSA gets served first.

There are many choices for finding and growing fresh, local, and healthy food. You can mix and match the ones that work best for you. Using your imagination to find ways to grow that work for you is part of the pleasure. And remember, this isn't hard! Gardening, eating, and enjoying the fresh air are all fun and healthy ways to spend your time.

Grow anywhere!

Resources

Amazing Above Ground Garden Kits
Yorktown, Texas 78164
261-491-0911
www.amazingabovegroundgarden.com

Boggy Creek Farm
Carol Ann Sayle and Larry Butler
3414 Lyons Road
Austin, TX 78702
512-926-4650
www.boggycreekfarm.com

Central Texas Gardener
Linda Lehmusvirta, producer, broadcast throughout Texas and beyond
www.klru.org/ctg

Community Gardens: To learn more and find out how to set up a community garden, visit www.communitygarden.org, the home of American Community Garden Association. To find gardens near you, search the Internet for community gardens and your city name.

Community Supported Agriculture: Visit www.localharvest.org/csa to learn how to choose a CSA and find a participating farm near you.

Friendly Aquaponics: Provides kits for sale as well as training and a regular newsletter plus free technical information and how-to info. Visit www.friendlyaquaponics.com.

Garden Anywhere Box
405-818-2599
www.gardenanywherebox.com

Haxnicks: Garden supplies, available at local nurseries or online at www.haxnicks.co.uk.

Highland Lakes Master Gardener Association, Texas: To see their Helping Garden and other projects, visit www.burnetcountyhighlandlakes mastergardener.org.

Master Gardener Program: To learn how to become a Master Gardener, contact the agriculture extension service in your county. Master Gardeners are active in all fifty states.

Pick Your Own: To find a farm near you that provides options for harvesting fresh food, visit www.pickyourown.org. This website provides information for farms in the United States and around the world.

The Poisoner's Handbook, by Deborah Blum, www.deborahblum. com. Order the book from your favorite bookseller and learn more about the PBS film, *The Poisoner's Handbook*, at www.pbs.org/wgbh/ americanexperience.

Renee's Garden
6060 Graham Hill Rd.
Felton, CA 95018
888-880-7228
www.reneesgarden.com
Seeds available in many local nurseries and online. Find a source for seeds near you online and also find tips for successful gardening, recipes, and plant information.

Index